Music Around the World

Music Around the World

Songs for a Global Classroom

by Jessica Gates Fredricks

Humanics Learning
Lake Worth, FL USA

Music Around the World
A Humanics Learning Publication

Humanics Learning
PO Box 1608
Lake Worth, FL 33460

© 2013 Second Edition
© 2003 by Brumby Holdings, LLC, 1st Edition

No part of this book may be reproduced or transmitted in any form or by any means, electronic or mechanical, including photocopying, recording, or by any information storage and retrieval system, without written permission from the publisher. For information, address Brumby.

Humanics Learning Publications are an imprint of and published by Humanics Publishing Group, a division of Brumby Holdings, LLC. It's trademark, consisting of the words "Humanics Learning" and a portrayal of a silhouetted girl, is registered in the U.S. Patent Office and in other countries.

Brumby Holdings, LLC
1197 Peachtree Street
Suite 533 Plaza
Atlanta, GA 30361

Printed in the United States of America

Library of Congress Control Number: 2002110792
ISBN (Paperback): 0-89334-379-X
ISBN (Hardcover): 0-89334-380-3

Table of Contents

Country	Music	Craft	Page
Australia	Lisbon Percy Grainger (from Lincolnshire Posy)	kangaroo puppet	1
Ireland	Derry Air (Danny Boy) Traditional	hanging shamrock	5
Japan	Bird Island Ryutaro Kaneko	weather journal	9
South Africa	Abantwana Basethempeleni Ladysmith Black Mambazo	conga drum	13
Germany	Finale from the Fifth Symphony Ludwig van Beethoven	frog hat, lily pad	17
Italy	Anvil Chorus Giuseppi Verdi (from Il Trovatore)	blacksmith hammer	21
Mexico	Granada Augustin Lara	tambourine	25
South Africa	Unhome Miriam Makeba	ankle rattle	30
United States	Hoedown Aaron Copland (from Rodeo)	cowboy vest	34
Brazil/Peru	Feijao com Pescao Meia Noite/Alex Acuna	bongos	38
Czech Republic	Finale from New World Symphony Antonin Dvorak	javelin, discus	42
Germany	Ride of the Valkyries Richard Wagner	shield, coat of arms	46

Country	Music	Craft	Page
Iran	Afshari Kamil Alipour	tabla drums	50
Italy	Spring Antonio Vivaldi (from The Four Seasons)	butterfly mask	54
Japan	Shake Tetsuro Naito	Japanese flag	58
Italy	William Tell Overture Gioacchino Rossini	sword, eye patch, mask	62
Norway	In the Hall of the Mountain King Edvard Grieg (from Peer Gynt)	mask	66
Russia	Samuel Goldenberg and Schmuyle Modeste Mussorgsky (from Pictures at an Exhibition)	wallet	70
Russia	1812 Overture Peter Tchaikovsky	bell and chain	74
Argentina	Malambo Alberto Ginastera (from Estancia)	planter	78
Austria	Surprise Symphony Joseph Haydn	shakers	82
China	Picking Flowers Traditional	spice bottles	86
England	Mars Gustav Holst (from The Planets)	mobile	90
France	March to the Scaffold Hector Berlioz (from Symphonie Fantastique)	arrow	94
Nigeria	Jewe Babatunde Olatunji	telescope	98

Country	Music	Craft	Page
Japan	Utuwaskarap Oki Kano	tankori, Ainu vest	102
Peru	Cumbias Traditional	Andean pan pipe	106
Peru	Redentor Alex Acuna	Meso-American temple	110
Russia	Gnomus Modeste Mussorgsky (from Pictures at an Exhibition)	balalaika	115
Russia	The Hut of Baba Yaga Modeste Mussorgsky (from Pictures at an Exhibition)	czar crown	119
Spain	La Virgen de la Macarena Traditional	rainstick	123

Common Core Standards Correlations   140

Introduction

This book contains 31 lesson plans that use music and movement activities to teach Core Knowledge science, math, geography and history skills. Each lesson plan includes a craft activity, movement activity and worksheet. The movement and craft activities are appropriate for all grade levels (K - 5). The worksheet is targeted specifically for the grade level listed under Core Connections at the top of each lesson plan. Above all — have fun!

Craft Activities

The following is a list of the craft materials students will use — most are recyclable materials that can be found around the house.

Paper towel tubes	Rubber bands	String or yarn	Brown paper grocery bags
Cereal boxes	Paper plates	Coat hangers	Plastic 2-liter bottles
Milk cartons	Dry rice or beans	Styrofoam cups	Scissors
Plastic milk caps	Tape or glue	Film canisters	Hole punch
Paper clips	Unlined white paper	Crayons or markers	Metal bottle caps
Construction paper	Paper lunch sacks	Toothpicks	Metal soda can flip-tops

Guidelines for Movement Activities

1. Convey to students that the music is all you want to hear during the activity. This not only develops good listening skills, it forces them to concentrate on the task at hand.

2. As the teacher, you must be the judge of how much movement is allowed, especially during free movement activities. The lesson plans are structured so that the story provides a basis for the movement activities, but there is a broad range of movements that can accompany each story. Some activities include free movement, meaning the students come up with their own movements instead of being led by the teacher. Keep in mind that some classes need more structure than others, either because of personalities or because of safety hazards in the classroom.

3. Make sure you have an immediate stop signal. The rule in my classroom is that when the music stops, the students stop: stop moving and stop talking. Practice the signal a few times — have the students walk around and chat, then give the signal. I tell my students that if they don't follow the signal, we don't move.

4. Familiarize yourself with the recording before you present each movement activity. If you know what's happening during the music, the students will have a more effective learning experience.

5. The lesson plans use a variety of music — everything from classical pieces that most everyone has heard to world music from the Far East. You'll find both you and your students saying "Oh, I know this one!" during some pieces, and "I never heard that before!" during others. It is important to know how the lesson plan fits with the music. Some of the stories involve acting out a specific story line: don't be shy! Approach the activities with enthusiasm and your students will follow.

Lisbon from Lincolnshire Posy
Percy Grainger
Australia

Core Connections

Kindergarten: Science — Animals and their Needs
> Animals, like plants, need food, water, and space to live and grow.
> Offspring are very much (but not exactly) like their parents.
> Most animal babies need to be fed and cared for by their parents.

Materials

Movement activity
Recording of Lincolnshire Posy
Map of Australia
Globe

Craft activity
Paper bag, scissors, tape or glue
Brown construction paper
Old magazines to cut pictures out of

Procedure

1. Show students a map of Australia and have them find the country on a globe.

2. Tell students the following story:

> Once there was kangaroo who was tired of living in the Australian outback. Her name was Sydney, and she had a mind of her own.
> "I want to live in the city," Sydney said. "I'm tired of living in the dirt."
> "Now, now," her father said. "You're still very young — just a baby kangaroo! And baby kangaroos need to be fed and cared for by their parents. You can't live in the city — who would take care of you?"
> Sydney narrowed her eyes. "I'm not a baby!"
> Father smiled. "No, you're not a baby, but you're still a very young kangaroo. And young kangaroos can get into lots of trouble when they live in the city by them-

selves."

"I can take care of myself."

Father sighed. "If you really want to live in the city, I can't stop you. But how will you get there?"

"I'll hop," said Sydney, heading out the door. "Isn't that what kangaroos do?"

And so Sydney set off by herself for the big city.

After a little while, she was thirsty and stopped at a water hole for a drink. She looked at herself in the reflection of the water.

"I'm not so little," she said. "I've got a pouch already."

"Whatcha doin over there?" came a small voice from behind her.

Sydney spun around to find a small lizard looking up at her. The lizard was small and brown and sunning himself on a large flat rock beside the water hole.

"I'm on my way to the big city," Sydney said.

"Whatcha gonna do there?" said the lizard, who looked very comfortable laying in the sun.

"I'm going to be a famous movie star, that's what."

The lizard blinked. "I ain't never heard of no famous kangaroos in the movies."

Sydney sniffed. "Well I'm going to be the first." And with that, she hopped off.

But before long she was thirsty again and stopped at another watering hole. She was enjoying a long drink when she heard a gruff voice behind her.

"What are you doing here?" The voice belonged to a large dog who looked mean.

"I'm having a drink of water on my way to the big city," Sydney said.

The dog barked, and seven more dogs appeared. "Do you know who I am?"

"No . . ."

"We're the Dingo Dogs, and we eat baby kangaroos! Let's get her, boys!"

The Dingos snarled and snapped at Sydney, but she was too quick for them. She hopped over the water hole and hopped as fast as she could, past the Dingo Dogs, past the lazy lizard, and all the way back to her home in the Australian outback.

And she was very happy.

3. Play the recording for students and ask them to close their eyes and imagine the story they have just heard as you describe what is happening according to the cue chart below.

4. Divide students into two groups: kangaroos and dingo dogs. Have the kangaroos sit on the ground in a circle with their puppets (from the craft activity) and the dogs against the wall. Make sure to leave space for the dogs to chase the puppets around the circle.

5. Go through the recording a second time, with students acting out their parts under your direction. Then have students switch parts so everyone gets a chance to be each part.

        :00   Sydney hops away from home
        :32   Dingo dogs chase Sydney
        :50   Sydney hops home, chased by dogs
      1:10   Sydney falls asleep at home

Craft Activity: Make a Kangaroo Puppet

Students can make a kangaroo puppet to use during the movement activity.

Teacher Preparation

Cut strips of brown construction paper that are 8 inches long by 2 inches wide. These will be folded accordion-style to make the kangaroo's arms and legs. Each student needs five strips — two arms, two legs, and one that will be cut in half to make the ears. Students will also need a 3-inch by 5-inch square of brown construction paper to use as the kangaroo's pouch. Each student needs a brown paper lunch sack for the body — you will need to show students how to put their hands in the folded sack for use as a puppet, with the bottom of the sack being the puppet's face.

Student Directions

1. Cut one of the brown paper strips in half and set it aside. Fold the other brown strips accordion-style and set them aside.

2. Have your teacher show you where to draw the kangaroo's face on the sack.

3. Glue an arm to each side of the sack. Then glue legs to the sack, low on each side.

4. Glue the kangaroo's pouch onto the front of the sack. Then glue on the ears.

Australia

Name _____

Kangaroos live in Australia. Australia is one of the seven continents.
Sydney wanted to live by herself, but most animal babies need to be fed and cared for by their parents.

Offsping look very much like their parents. Cut out pictures of animals and their babies and paste them below.

Humans are animals. Animals need things to live:

Food	**Water**	**Space to live and grow**
Draw your favorite food.	Draw yourself drinking water.	Draw a picture of where you live.

© 2003 Humanics Learning. From *Music Around the World* by Jessica Gates Fredricks

Derry Air (Danny Boy)
Ireland
Traditional

Core Connections

Kindergarten: World Geography — Seven Continents
Identify and locate the seven continents on a map and globe
Asia
Europe
Africa
North America
South America
Antarctica
Australia

Materials

Movement activity
Recording of Derry Air (Danny Boy)
Map of Ireland
Globe

Craft activity
Green construction paper
Paper plates
Glue, scissors, pencils
Paper clips, yarn, hole punch

Procedure

1. Show students a map of Ireland and have them find the country on a globe.

2. Tell students the following story:
    A long time ago in Ireland there was a young boy named Danny who wanted to be a sailor. Now, this was not unusual because Ireland is an island, which means it is surrounded by water on all sides.
    But this young boy's mother did not want him to become a sailor, for she had heard that many of the young men who became sailors often did not come home, and

if her son did not come home she would be very sad, for she loved him very much.

Danny's mother hoped that as he grew older, he would stop dreaming about becoming a sailor and want to grow up to be something else — a scientist, or a doctor, or even a potato farmer. Potato farming was big business in Ireland — everybody grew potatoes, and a good potato farmer could make lots and lots of money.

But Danny was not interested in money.

Danny's mother hoped, that even if her son was not interested in having lots and lots of money, that he would be interested in meeting a fine lady and buying a house of their own, where they would live happily and have many fine children, and then Danny would know why his mother did not want him to go.

But Danny was not interested in having a family of his own.

Danny was only interested in being a sailor. And on his 18th birthday, he packed all his meager clothes into a canvas sack, kissed his mother good-bye and boarded a ship to learn the business of sailing.

It was the last time Danny's mother ever saw him, for Danny loved the sea so much that he never came home. He was content to ride the waves around the great oceans of the world, seeing new sights and writing letters home in every port.

And though Danny's mother was sad that her son left, she was glad that he was getting to see the world. She wanted to tell all of Ireland of her wonderful son, and so would from time to time hum a little tune. And her neighbors would ask what she was humming, and she would smile and say: "It's just my Danny boy".

Eventually her neighbors began to learn the tune, and soon all of Ireland was singing the song — for everybody knew someone who had become a sailor and no longer lived on the island.   And the song is still sung today.

3. Play the recording and ask students how it makes them feel. (sleepy, sad, etc.)

4. Play the recording a second time and have students mirror your motions as you follow the cue chart below:

   Oh Danny boy, the pipes the pipes are calling (put hand to ear as if listening)
   from glen to glen, and down the mountainside (make mountain with hands)
   the summer's gone, and all the flowers are dying (make motions for falling rose petals)
   tis you, tis you, must go and I must bide (kneel with head bowed)

   But come ye back when summer's in the meadow (stand, put arm out and turn in a circle)
   And all the valley's hushed and white with snow (close eyes, cross hands over chest)
   Tis I'll be here in sunshine or in shadow (make sunbeam motions, then curl in a little ball)
   Oh Danny boy, oh Danny boy I love you so (draw a heart in the air)

Craft Activity: Make a Hanging Shamrock

Shamrocks are a symbol of Ireland — along with leprechauns and the pot of gold at the end of the rainbow. Students can make a hanging shamrock for the classroom.

Teacher Preparation

Each student needs one sheet of green construction paper. They will cut the paper into four parts that will become the four leaves of the shamrock. You need to have small strips of green construction paper cut for the stem of the shamrock.

Student Directions

1. Fold your piece of construction paper in half, and then fold it in half again.

2. Place your hand — fingers closed — on the paper and trace it with a pencil.

3. Cut out the shape of your hand before opening the paper — you should have four hand-shaped pieces of green paper. These are the leaves of your shamrock.

4. Glue the leaves of your shamrock onto the paper plate and ask your teacher for a stem piece to glue onto the bottom of the shamrock.

5. Ask your teacher to punch a hole in the top of the paper plate, thread the hole with yarn, and hang it from the ceiling with a paper clip.

Ireland

Name _____

Ireland is a country in Europe. Europe is one of seven continents on the globe.

On the map below:

    Find **Africa** and color it red
    Find **Asia** and color it brown
    Find **Europe** and color it yellow
    Find **North America** and color it green
    Find **South America** and color it orange
    Find **Australia** and color it blue
    Find **Antarctica** and color it purple

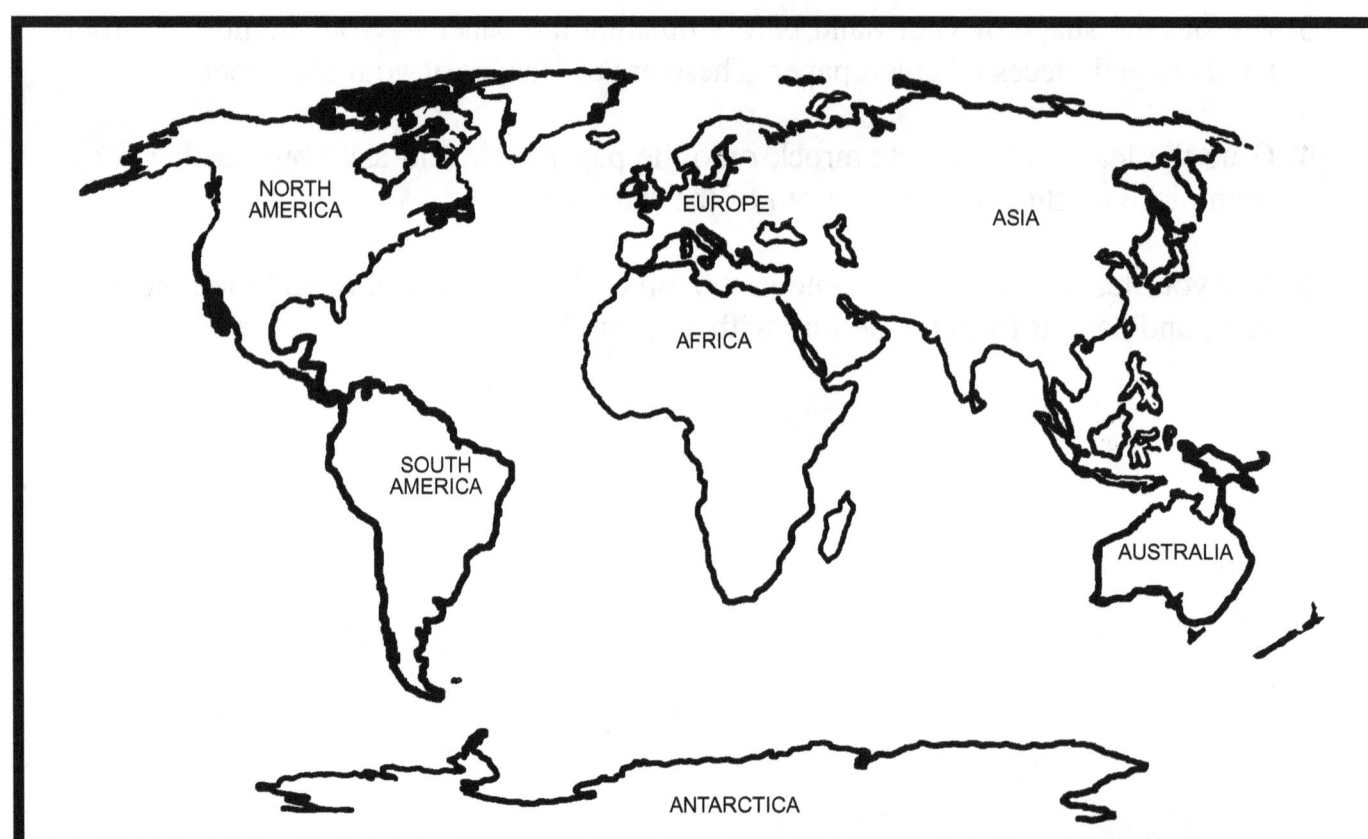

© 2003 Humanics Learning. From *Music Around the World* by Jessica Gates Fredricks

Bird Island
Ryutaro Kaneko
Japan

Core Connections

Kindergarten: Seasons and Weather
        The four seasons
        Rainfall: how the condition of the ground varies with rainfall

Materials

Movement activity
Recording of Bird Island
Map of Japan
Globe

Craft activity
Crayons or markers
Unlined white paper
Stapler

Procedure

1. Show students a map of Japan and have them find the country on a globe.

2. Tell students the following story:

    In a tiny village on the island of Japan, there was a young boy. Now, this boy was the youngest boy in his village. He was not only the youngest, but he was also the smallest. The other children teased him mercilessly. They called him "bird", because they said he was so tiny he must be a bird.

    In time the villagers forgot his real name and soon everyone called him Bird, because they heard him called that so much that eventually it became true.

    Bird was indeed small, but he was also very smart. He saw how they lived on an island, and how the waves sometimes became so large that they would wash into the village. Sometimes the waves were so strong that they even carried houses away.

    Bird did not want his house to wash away, so he built it up on stilts. The villagers shook their heads and laughed, saying: "That one is rightly named, Bird. Look how he builds his house high up in the air, as if he is trying to live in the skies as a bird!"

And so the villagers laughed in the fall, while the rains were slight. They saw how Bird had to climb a ladder every time he wanted to get into his house instead of just walking in like they did. They said: "Bird is crazy."

And the villagers laughed in the winter, while there was no rain. They saw how Bird shivered from the whipping winds because he had no trees to protect him. They said: "Bird is crazy."

And the villagers laughed in spring, while the rains began again. They saw how Bird had to share his house with the winged animals because the house was up so high the winged animals thought it was part of a mountain! They said: "Bird is crazy."

But when summer came, the villagers didn't have time to laugh. For summer was the time of the great rains and great waves. At first it was just a little rain, and very tiny waves, and the villagers said: "This is just a little rain, and the waves are not so big, and it will stop soon."

And Bird looked down at them from his high and dry house and smiled.

But it did not stop. And the ground was so full it could not swallow any more rain, so the rain lay on the ground as deep as a man's foot, with tiny waves riding on top.

After a month the villagers said: "This is a lot of rain, but it will stop soon."

And Bird looked down on them from his high and dry house and smiled.

But it did not stop. And the rain on the ground grew higher and higher until it was as deep as a man's knee. And this would not have been so bad, but the waves on top grew larger by the day, until there was so much water that the entire village — except for Bird's house, for his house was on stilts so high that no waves could reach it — washed into the sea!

As the houses washed away, the villagers cried and cried, for now they had no place to live.

And Bird looked down on them from his high and dry house and smiled.

3. Divide the students into two groups: Bird and villagers. Try to have more villagers than Bird(s). Run through the piece and cue each group as listed. (When one group is moving, the other remains still.) After the first run-through, have the students switch parts so everyone gets a chance to be each character.

    :00   Villagers building houses
    :14   Villagers dancing in fall (flutes)
    :41   Villagers teasing Bird (clapping)
    :55   Villagers dancing in winter (flutes)
    1:08   Villagers teasing Bird (clapping)
    1:21   Villagers dancing in spring (flutes and clapping)

1:34 Villagers teasing Bird
1:47 Rains of summer, villagers look up
2:14 Rain sweeps houses away, Bird does dance

Craft Activity: Make a Weather Journal

Students can make a weather journal to record their local weather changes. This can be used to teach students how to read a thermometer. Give them simple things to draw — rain drops if it's rainy, or a sun if it's sunny, or clouds if it's cloudy — each day and have them record the temperature. Students can also cut pictures from a magazine and glue them into their weather journals to show what's happening in their area.

Teacher Preparation

Cut sheets of paper in quarters and staple 10 together to make monthly weather journals for each student.

Student Directions

1. Put your name on the front of your weather journal.

2. Decorate the front of your weather journal with crayons or markers.

3. Record the weather each day by drawing what you see and recording the temperature!

4. Try finding weather pictures in magazines — then cut them out and paste them in your journal!

Weather

Name _____
Date _____

There are four seasons in a year.
Fall is a change from hot to cold. Leaves change color in the Fall. Draw some leaves below.

Winter is very cold. In some places it snows. Snowflakes fall when it snows in Winter. Draw some snowflakes below.

Spring is a change from cold to hot. Flowers bloom in the Spring. Draw some flowers below.

Summer is very hot. In some places it rains. The sun is very bright in the Summer. Draw a sun below.

© 2003 Humanics Learning. From *Music Around the World* by Jessica Gates Fredricks

Abantwana Basethempeleni
Ladysmith Black Mambazo
South Africa

Core Connections

Kindergarten: Science — The Human Body
　　　　The five senses and associated body parts:
　　　　Sight: eyes
　　　　Hearing: ears
　　　　Smell: nose
　　　　Taste: tongue
　　　　Touch: skin

Materials

Movement activity
Recording of Abantwana Basethempeleni
Map of South Africa and Africa
Globe

Craft activity
5-gallon plastic bucket
White paper and glue
Crayons or markers

Procedure

1. Show students a map of Africa and South Africa. Point out that South Africa is a country while Africa is a continent and help them find both on a globe.

2. Tell students the following story:

　　Once upon a time in South Africa there was a little boy who wanted to make music. He heard his father and mother and sister making music all day long and wanted to be part of it more than anything else in the world. But no one ever told him how. He waited and waited until he couldn't wait anymore. He went to his father and said: "Father, how do you make music?"

Father smiled, for the boy was very young and did not yet understand the ways of the world, and said: "My son, music is already here — you do not have to make it."

And the boy was very confused. So he went to his mother and said: "Mother, how do you make music?"

Mother smiled, for although the boy was very young and did not yet understand the ways of the world, he understood that music was important, so she said: "My son, music is here and there, and you must listen to hear it calling your name."

And the boy was very confused. So he went to his sister and said: "Sister, how do you make music?"

Sister smiled, for although she was only four years older than him, she knew that music is something wonderful indeed, something that her mother would have called special, and remembered wanting to know how it was made, and she said: "My brother, when you ask how music is made, you are speaking so loudly that you cannot hear the music itself."

And the boy was very confused. He was also very unhappy because he had hoped that his own family would at least help him learn to make music.

The boy felt very alone — if his own family wouldn't help him learn music, then who would? He was so sad, he was sad sad, and even some would say he was sad sad sad. The boy sat down on a stone near the kapok tree to be alone with his misery.

His eyes saw the tall savannah grasses blowing in the breeze. Back and forth, back and forth, back and forth. And his bare feet began to tap in time with the grasses, *back and forth, back and forth, back and forth.*

The skin on his bare feet felt the roughness of the sand between his toes. The grains ground against each other as he tapped with the grasses and made a soft sound, like the tiny wings of a moth beating against the wind. *Whup whup whup, whup whup whup, whup whup whup.*

His mouth began to water as the wind changed direction, bringing the smell of roasting meat from a nearby hut right into his nose — he could almost taste the meat on his tongue!

His ears heard the soft *thump-thump-thump-thump* of a hyena's fast feet as it was shooed away from the smell of roasting meat.

And suddenly the boy realized he could hear the music around him.

Thump-thump-thump-thump
    Back and forth, back and forth, back and forth
        Whup whup whup, whup whup whup, whup whup, whup

The boy ran home to tell his father, mother, and sister, for he was not sad sad sad anymore — on the contrary, he was now happy happy happy!

3. When you finish the story, ask if anyone heard anything that sounded weird. (sad sad or happy happy). Explain to the students that South African storytellers will simply

repeat a word if they want to emphasize something. So instead of saying *very happy*, they would say *happy happy*.

4. Play the recording and ask students if they can hear the sounds of the African wilderness in the music. Tell students that you are going to do a circle dance. This is where you stand in a circle and everyone steps to the beat. Then someone steps into the circle and does a special move, like turning around, or putting their hands in the air, and everyone in the circle follows their lead. Invite students to stand up in a circle and step to the beat of the music. Stand in the center of the circle and lead them in mirroring motions — if you have time, invite a student to lead the group.

Craft Activity: Make a Conga Drum

The conga drum is one of the largest African hand drums. They are usually made out of wood and are very expensive, but you can make one out of an empty 5-gallon plastic bucket. These can be purchased at hardware stores, but the easiest way to get them is to drop by a construction site and ask for some empty ones — contractors usually throw them away and are happy to get rid of them!

Teacher preparation

Have students bring in a 5-gallon plastic bucket.

Student directions

1. Turn the bucket upside-down. The bottom of the bucket is now the drum head. Then cover the sides of your bucket with white paper and decorate it with crayons.

2. Experiment with your conga drum to find all the different sounds — try fingertips on the sides and palms of the hands in the very center of the drum head.

The Five Senses

Name _____
Date _____

The human body has five senses:
You see with your eyes. Draw something you see below.

You hear with your ears. Draw something you hear below.

You smell with your nose. Draw something you smell below.

You taste with your tongue. Draw something you taste below.

You touch with your skin. Draw something you touch below.

© 2003 Humanics Learning. From *Music Around the World* by Jessica Gates Fredricks

Jessica Gates Fredricks / 17

Finale from the Fifth Symphony
Ludwig van Beethoven
Germany

Core Connections

Grades 1 and 2: Find directions on a map — east, west, north, south
Review the seven continents

Materials

Movement activity
Recording of Fifth Symphony
Map of Germany
Globe

Craft activity
Green construction paper
4 Paper plates
Glue sticks
Green crayons or markers

Procedure

1. Show students a map of Germany and have them find the country on a globe.

2. Tell students the following story:

   Once upon a time there were two frogs in a pond.
   The first frog said, "I'm the best frog in the pond, so I'm going to teach you how to jump."
   The second frog said, "No, that can't be, because I'm the best frog in the pond. I will teach you how to jump."
   The frogs stared at one another and frowned. The first frog said, "I am the best frog in the pond, and I can prove it."
   "Oh yeah? Then prove it," said the second frog.
   "The best frog in the pond will have the loudest voice," said the first frog. "Listen to this." And with that the first frog took a big breath and yelled, "I am a frog!"

The second frog stuck his tongue out. "That's nothing," he said. "Listen to this." And the second frog took an even bigger breath and yelled "I am a frog!"

The frogs stared at one another and frowned. The second frog said. "This isn't working. I have a better idea."

"Oh yeah? Then prove it," said the first frog.

"The best frog in the pond will be able to jump the highest," said the second frog. "Watch this." And with that the second frog bent his legs and got very close to the ground. He jumped three times, one, two three, with each jump bigger than the last.

The first frog stuck his tongue out. "That's nothing," he said. "Watch this." And with that the first frog bent his legs and got even closer to the ground. He jumped three times, one, two three, with each jump bigger than the last.

After that both frogs were very tired indeed, and they stopped arguing to catch their breaths.

And when they did, they saw that all the other frogs in the pond were watching them with wide eyes. Suddenly the very tiniest frog came hop, hop, hopping towards them.

The first frog called to him. "Little frog, why is every frog staring at us?"

The little frog answered, "We heard you both croaking louder than any other frog, and when we came to see what was wrong, we saw you both jumping higher than any other frog. So we know you both must be the best frogs in the pond."

The two frogs stared at each other . . . and smiled. It seemed the pond could have two best frogs after all.

3. Divide students into two groups (first frog, second frog) and have the groups face each other. Play the recording and tell students the two opening statements of the theme are the first frog yelling "I am a frog!" and then the second frog yelling it back. Play just this first part and have the students practice yelling in time with the music.

4. After they have the opening statement, lead all students in saying the following pattern in time with the music: jump, jump, jump, breathe. Repeat this pattern three times, and the fourth time slow the pattern in time with the music. Then all frogs say "I am a frog" with the music.

5. Once students can say their parts, have them perform their parts, making sure the two groups are staring at each other.

Craft Activity: Make a Frog Hat and Lily Pad

Students can make a frog hat to use during the movement activity, and you can turn the room into a frog pond by having each student make lily pads that they can stand on during the movement activity.

Teacher preparation

Have each student bring in four paper plates. Each student will make one big lily pad using the four plates. You can make a frog hat using a piece of green construction paper. Make a diagonal cut from one corner to the center of the paper. Then fold or bend the paper to make a cone-shaped hat. Students can decorate the hats with wiggly eyes if available, or draw eyes with crayons.

Student directions

1. Color the four paper plates green.

2. Use a glue stick to attach your four paper plates together in the shape of a four-leaf clover. This will be your lily pad.

3. Draw or glue eyes onto the piece of green paper your teacher gives you. Then follow your teacher's directions to fold the paper into a hat.

4. Place your lily pad on the floor, then put on your hat. Perform the movement activity again, and remember to land on the lily pad when you jump!

Germany

Name _____

Germany is a country in Europe. Europe is one of seven continents on the globe. The other six continents are: **North America, South America, Asia, Antarctica, Australia,** and **Africa**.

To find Antarctica, go **south** to the very bottom of the map.
To find Asia, go **east** of Europe.
To find South America, go **west** of Africa.
To find Australia, go **north** of Antarctica.

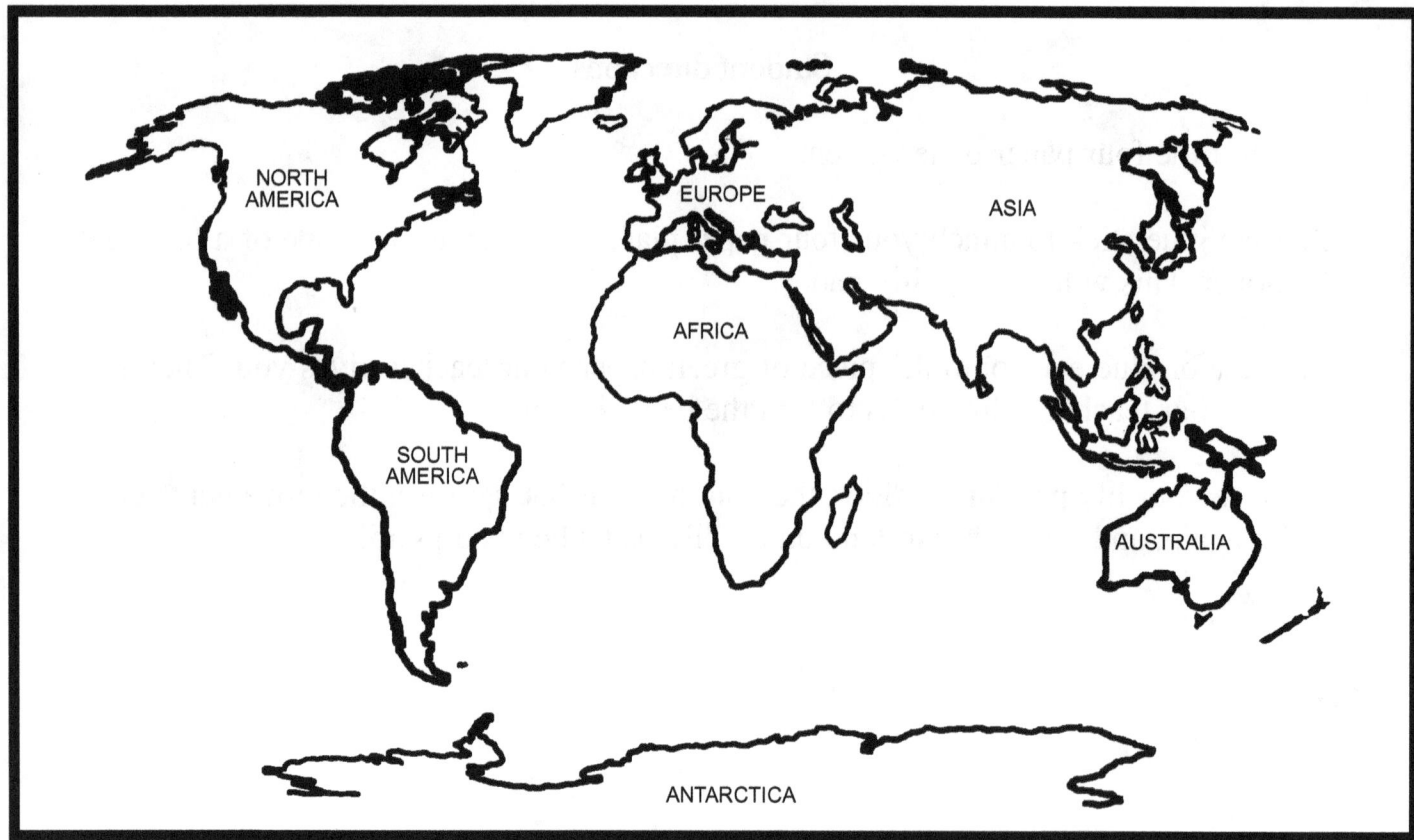

On the map, color **North America** blue. Color **South America** red. Color **Australia** green. Color **Asia** black. Color **Europe** brown. Color **Africa** purple. Color **Antarctica** yellow.

© 2003 Humanics Learning. From *Music Around the World* by Jessica Gates Fredricks

Jessica Gates Fredricks

Anvil Chorus from *Il Trovatore*
Giuseppi Verdi
Italy

Core Connections

Grades 1, 2 and 3: Geography terms
                peninsula, island
Grade 3: Geography of the Mediterranean Region (ancient Rome)
                Mediterranean Sea, Greece, Italy, France, Spain, Black Sea, Atlantic Ocean

Materials

Movement activity
Recording of Anvil Chorus
Rulers or other hammer-like prop
Map of Italy
Globe

Craft activity
Paper towel tubes
Milk carton
masking tape
colored paper (black and brown)

Procedure

1. Show students a map of Italy and have them find the country on a globe.

2. Tell students the following story:

     A long time ago in Italy there used to be small magical creatures called dwarves. The dwarves worked with metal — silver and gold — to create weapons for mighty armies because everybody knew the dwarves had a knack for metalworking. Any metal worked by the dwarves had special powers — maybe a sword blade that never got dull, or an arrowhead that always found its mark.
     At one time a very evil king took over the land where the dwarves lived and forced them to work night and day. Even when the dwarves took a break to eat lunch, the evil king chased them back to work.

The dwarves often complained about the work by stomping hard on the floor, and sometimes they would stop walking entirely. They could usually only get away with this twice before the evil king's guards made the dwarves run all the way back to the metal shop. This didn't stop the dwarves from complaining about their work before kneeling down and working with the metal.

Dwarves work with very hot metal. They place the metal on an anvil and beat it with hammers to shape it into swords and other weapons. Dwarves are always careful when they work with metal — they only hit the metal directly in front of them and never hit any other dwarves. Not even on accident! That's how careful dwarves are.

3. Four different movements are used in this song: stomping, running, dwarves complaining, and dwarves working with metal. Before listening, discuss what kind of qualities (loud, soft, fast, etc.) each activity might sound like. Tell students they will hear actual anvils being hit with hammers during the song. The song sequence is:

Dwarves stomping (timpani—students stomp around room in a circle)
Stop
Dwarves stomping
Stop
Dwarves running (triangle 8th's—jog in circle)
Dwarves complaining (people singing, yelling—look angry, wave arms)
Kneel on shouts and get ready to work anvils
Dwarves working the metal (hit floor in time with anvils in music)
Dwarves complaining
2 hits
Dwarves stomping (timpani)
Stop
Dwarves stomping
Stop
Dwarves running (triangle 8th's)
Working the metal (Hit floor with anvils in music)
Dwarves complaining (look angry, kneel)
2 hits

4. Once students can identify the aural cues, give each student a ruler or other hammer-like prop and have them act it out under the teacher's direction.

Craft Activity: Make a Blacksmith's Hammer

People who work with metal are called blacksmiths. The dwarves in the story might also be called blacksmiths. Blacksmith hammers are not like the ones we use to hammer nails into a wall — they are solid blocks of metal on wooden handles. Blacksmiths heat the metal to be worked until it is at a very high temperature before placing the metal on an iron anvil and beating it into the proper shape.

In the Anvil Chorus, the composer wrote in parts for anvils. What the students hear during the piece is an actual anvil being hit with a hammer. This activity allows them to make a hammer that looks like a tool a blacksmith might use.

Teacher preparation

Have students bring in empty paper towel rolls and empty milk cartons. Make sure the milk cartons are washed and dried before using. Cut off the pouring end of the milk carton so the carton forms a rectangle. Then cut holes in the side of the milk carton so the paper towel tube can pass through. The tube is the hammer handle and the milk carton is the hammer head.

Student directions

1. Put the cardboard tube through the holes in the milk carton. Make sure about one inch of the tube is sticking out the top of the milk carton.

2. Use masking tape to secure the tube to the carton. Place tape where the tube and carton join outside the carton first, and then place tape at the joints inside the carton. Make sure the carton is secure!

3. Cover the milk carton with black paper. This will be the head of your hammer.

4. Cover the cardboard tube with brown paper. This will be the handle of your hammer.

5. Do the movement activity again, and this time use your own hammer.

Italy

Name _____
Date _____

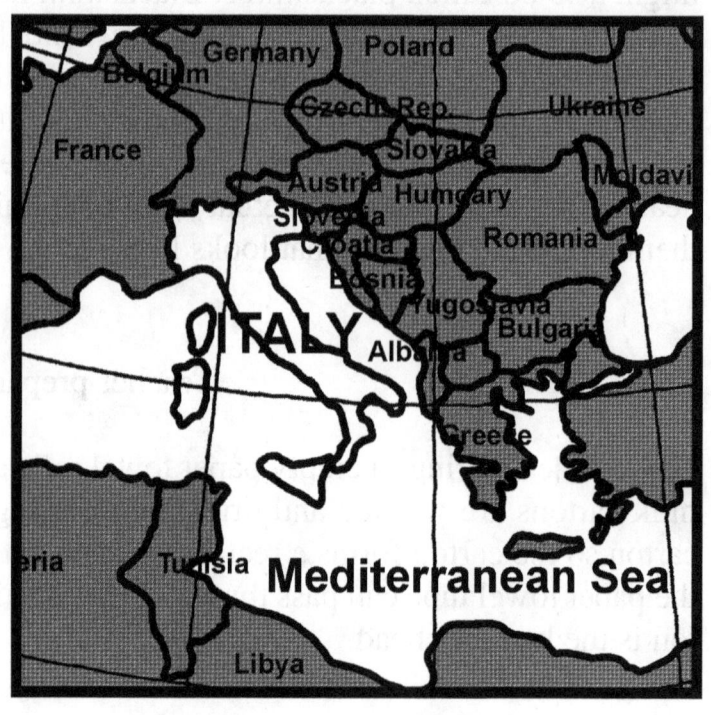

Italy is a country in Europe. The **Mediterranean Sea** surrounds Italy. This makes Italy a **peninsula**, because it is surrounded by water on three sides.

Below Italy is the island of Sicily. An **island** is surrounded by water on all sides.

The Mediterranean Sea is not the only body of water on the map. There are two others.

The **Atlantic Ocean** is in the northwest corner of the map. Color it blue.

A part of the **Black Sea** is also on your map. It is in the northeast part of the map. Find it and color it blue.

Italy is surrounded by many countries. If you look east of Italy, you will see **Greece**. Color it green.

If you look west of Italy, you will see **Spain**. Color Spain red.

If you look northwest of Italy, you will see **France**. Color France orange.

The Italian flag was adopted in 1870. It uses three colors: green, white, and red. Color the flag below. Make the first stripe green, leave the middle stripe white, and color the last stripe red.

Answer the questions.

1. A peninsula has water on _____ sides.

2. A _____ is completely surrounded by water.

3. The _____ Sea surrounds Italy.

© 2003 Humanics Learning. From *Music Around the World* by Jessica Gates Fredricks

Granada
Augustin Lara
Mexico

Core Connections

Grade 1: Mexico — Geography
        North American continent: locate Mexico relative to the U.S.
        Yucatan Peninsula
        Pacific Ocean, Gulf of Mexico, Rio Grande
        Mexico City

Materials

Movement activity
Recording of Granada
Map of Mexico
Globe

Craft activity
Two paper plates
10 metal bottle caps
Hammer, nail
Glue, crayons, pipe cleaners

Procedure

1. Show students a map of Mexico and have them find the country on a globe.

2. Tell students the following story:

     Once upon a time there was a tiny village on the Yucatan Peninsula that was immune to time. Somehow, the world grew old around it and no one in the village — not mothers or fathers or sisters or brothers or aunts or uncles or grandmothers or grandfathers or even dogs or cats! — grew even the slightest bit older.
     No one in the village knew anything was wrong, of course — how could they? To them it seemed as if everything was going along fine, and no one knew anything was wrong until a young girl got lost while searching for her pet bird in the jungle. The girl's name was Maria, and her bird was a very beautiful quetzal named Emelio.

Emelio loved to eat the large mosquitos that flitted through the jungle, and Maria always took him to the jungle once a day so he could hunt mosquitos. But on this day, she was distracted from watching Emelio by footprints she found on the ground.

Now footprints were not that unusual in the jungle, but these particular footprints didn't look like any she'd seen — where were the toes? It was just one big foot!

So Maria followed the footprints until she came to a small clearing in the jungle and here she found an interesting sight — many small metal cans, with a hole in the top as if to drink out of. What in the world are these, Maria wondered, for although she had heard of such things, she had never seen one in real life. The cans had strange writing on the side, with letters she knew but the words made no sense. C-o-k-e. What was that?

Suddenly, Maria heard voices. They were very far away but they were definitely voices. She followed the sound of the voices until she came to the end of the jungle — she hadn't even known the jungle had an end! — and peeked out behind a banana tree.

Maria couldn't believe her eyes.

In front of her were the largest huts she'd ever seen! Huge pyramid-shaped buildings that rose miles into the sky! And all made of stone — the huts in her village were made of wood.

Maria took a tentative step onto the street — it was also made of stone — and walked towards the many people who were gathered in the middle of the street.

"Welcome to the plaza," said a woman, smiling at her. "What can we do for you today?"

Maria stared at her. "What is this place?"

"This is the plaza, mi amiga. All of Mexico City brings items here to sell. You can find fresh fruit, the finest cloth, and mariachi music — we have everything your heart desires."

Maria began to walk among the shops, feeling the fine cloth and smelling the delicious aromas of the roasting fish. But she stopped in her tracks when she heard the musicians of the mariachi band play — such amazing sounds from such tiny men!

Maria began to wonder if she would ever want to go back to her village after seeing the wonderful sights of Mexico City. But as she looked around, Maria realized that she didn't know anyone in the Plaza. She had no family and no friends — she couldn't even find Emelio!

And so she ran back to her village in the Yucutan. To this day, residents of Mexico City talk of the young wide-eyed girl who visited the plaza and loved their city, but still returned home because of her one true love — her family.

3. Play the recording and tell students what's happening according to the cue chart.

4. Divide students into the following groups: Emelio, mosquitos, Maria, plaza vendors, mariachi musicians. Give each group a specific posture to maintain during the activity.

5. After the groups have learned their postures, play the piece a second time and have students act it out under your direction according to the cue chart below.

       :00   Emelio hunts mosquitos near Maria
       :56   Maria follows footprints
      1:26   Maria finds soda cans
      1:48   Maria hears voices and follows it to Mexico City plaza
      2:08   Maria reaches Mexico City plaza and stares
      2:35   Maria strolls among shops
      3:17   Maria listens to mariachi band
      4:15   Maria runs back to Yucutan

Craft Activity: Make a Tambourine

Tambourines are a staple of Mexican mariachi music. Students can make one using two paper plates and metal bottle caps. Note: paper clips may be susbstituted for caps.

Teacher preparation

Have students bring in two paper plates and 10 metal bottle caps (or 20 paper clips). Use the hammer to flatten the bottle caps before punching a hole in each one with a nail.

Student directions

1. Turn the paper plates upside down and decorate them with crayons.

2. Glue the paper plates together so there is space in the middle and the outer rims touch.

3. Get your teacher to punch five holes around the rim of the tambourine. Thread a pipe cleaner through each hole, then through two flattened bottle caps. Twist the pipe

cleaner closed.

4. Shake your tambourine to the mariachi music!

Mexico

Name _____
Date _____

Mexico is a country on the continent of North America. It is south of the United States. The capital of Mexico is Mexico City.

Circle the correct answer.

1. What continent is Mexico on?

South America   North America   Africa

2. What is the capital of Mexico?

Mexico City   Capital City   Washington D.C.

On the map below:
    Find the **Yucutan Peninsula** and color it yellow
    Find the **Pacific Ocean** and color it blue
    Find the **Gulf of Mexico** and color it green
    Find the **Rio Grande** river and trace it with a red crayon
    Find **Mexico City** and draw a brown box around it

© 2003 Humanics Learning. From *Music Around the World* by Jessica Gates Fredricks

Unhome
Miriam Makeba
South Africa

Core Connections

Grade 1: Science — Special Classifications of Animals
      Herbivores: plant-eaters (elephants, cows, deer)
      Carnivores: flesh-eaters (lions, tigers)
      Omnivores: plant and animal-eaters (bears)

Materials

Movement activity
Recording of Unhome
Map of South Africa
Globe
ankle rattle from craft activity

Craft activity
Construction paper
Tape, crayons
Eight plastic milk caps
Dry rice or beans

Procedure

1. Show students a map of South Africa and have them find the country on a globe. Be sure to make the distinction that Africa is a continent while South Africa is a country.

2. Tell students the following story:

    On the plains of South Africa lived a pride of lions. Lions are carnivores and this means that they eat other animals. The other animals of the plain were always careful to stay away from the lion pride as much as possible.
    Except for Juluka.
    Juluka was the smallest brown hyena in his family. He had not yet lost his spots

that all baby hyenas have to make them blend into the surrounding plains, and the other hyena children teased him.

"Look at Juluka," said the oldest hyena child, who was not very nice at all and was called Masekela by the other children. "See how he is still a baby with his many spots!"

"I can't," said another of the older children, this one a female named Kenya, "he has so many spots that I can't see him at all!"

And though they were brown hyenas and not actually laughing hyenas like their cousins in the Kalahari Desert, Kenya and Masekela would fall to the ground, laughing.

Now, Juluka had a mind to tell the mean ones — as some of the children called them behind their backs — that he would rather disappear because of his spots than be mistaken for a laughing hyena, for everyone knew that a laughing hyena was the absolute lowest hyena in all of Africa. This was so because laughing hyenas usually laughed so hard that they never had time for anything else — no work, no play, just uncontrollable laughing — and as such they were considered the lowest of the low.

But that would have only made the mean ones angry and Juluka had no intention of making things worse. True, he was still spotted, but there was nothing he could do about that — the spots would change as he grew bigger and no amount of wishing would make them go. But Masekela and Kenya could certainly do something about acting like laughing hyenas!

From the brush behind him, Juluka heard a low growl. The fur on the back of his neck bristled, and instinctively he sank low to the ground.

Lions!

Peeking through the grass, Juluka saw a mother lion and her two cubs — all three looking very hungry — growling softly to themselves as they stared at their next meal. But they weren't staring at Juluka — his spots made him blend right into the brush!

The lions were staring at the mean ones.

Kenya and Masekela were still rolling in the dirt, laughing at Juluka's spots and looking for all the world like laughing hyenas.

Laughing hyenas were the lowest of the low for a reason — they were the loudest and easiest to find when a hungry lion was looking for a quick meal.

The three lions pounced on Kenya and Masekela — who made a quick meal indeed for the hungry lions — and then went off to lie in the sun.

Juluka crept back to his mother's den. He guessed that having spots wasn't so bad after all.

3. Play the recording of Unhome and this time, read the story as the music plays. Begin reading when Makeba begins singing and try to make the story last four minutes. At

about 4:08 on the recording, students should mirror you as you move to the music.

4. Play the recording of Unhome a second time, again reading the story, and have the children form a circle around you, wearing their ankle rattles. They will march in a circle around you as you tell the story to the music, and when it's done they will mirror your movements as before.

Craft Activity: Make an Ankle Rattle

Natives of the Zulu tribe often wear ankle rattles when they dance. The rattles are made from dried goat's hooves that are strung onto a wide piece of leather. The leather is then tied around the ankle and used during ceremonies. Students can make an ankle rattle using eight milk caps, dry beans or rice, construction paper and lots of tape.

Teacher preparation

Have students bring in eight milk caps to make the rattles for their ankle rattle.

Student directions

1. First make the rattles. Take four milk caps and place them on the table upside-down so that the open end is up.

2. Put some dry rice or beans in each cap — don't make them too full or you won't get much sound out of the rattle.

3. Finish the rattle by putting the empty caps on top of the filled caps and securing them together with tape. You should be able to pick the rattle up and shake it to hear the sound without any rice or beans coming out.

4. Now fold a piece of construction paper in half long-ways and tape the rattles securely to the construction paper. Decorate the paper with crayons.

5. Get your teacher to help you tape the ankle rattle to your ankle and get ready to use it in the movement activity!

Animals

Name _____
Date _____

Animals are often classified by what they eat.

Herbivores eat plants. A cow is an herbivore. Draw a cow below.

Carnivores eat meat. A lion is a carnivore. Draw a lion below.

Omnivores eat plants and meat. A bear is a carnivore. Draw a bear below.

Circle the correct answer.
1. Humans eat plants and meat. They are _____.
       herbivores   carnivores   omnivores

2. Elephants eat plants. They are _____.
       herbivores   carnivores   omnivores

3. Tigers eat meat. They are _____.
       herbivores   carnivores   omnivores

© 2003 Humanics Learning. From *Music Around the World* by Jessica Gates Fredricks

Hoedown
Aaron Copland
United States

Core Connections

Grade 1: Geography of the American West
            Appalachian Mountains, Rocky Mountains, Mississippi River
            North America, Atlantic Ocean, Pacific Ocean, East, West, North, South

Materials

Movement activity
Recording of Hoedown
Map of United States
Globe

Craft activity
Brown paper bag
Crayons

Procedure

1. Show students a map of the United States and have them find the country on a globe. Have them locate the state in which they live, and the state of New Mexico.

2. Tell students the following story:

    Have you ever been in a very dark room? A room so dark that when you held you hand in front of your face, you couldn't see it?
    Jim White has. Jim was a teenage cowboy who lived 100 years ago. He lived in southeastern New Mexico, near a town called Carlsbad. Carlsbad was surrounded by the Chihuahuan Desert, a place Jim loved to explore.
    One evening as he was riding his horse home, Jim saw hundreds of bats flying out of a hole in the ground. When he rode closer to investigate, he saw the hole was huge and had very steep sides. He couldn't see the bottom, but he still wanted to explore it.
    The next day Jim returned with rope and climbed down into the hole. After a few

minutes he came to the end of his rope. He couldn't see the top of the hole anymore. It was so dark he couldn't see his hands or the rope. He heard soft rustling sounds — bats! Even though he couldn't see the bats, Jim knew they were there.

Jim was scared — he couldn't see anything and he heard lots of strange sounds. Part of him wanted to climb out and ride away from the hole. But another part of him wanted to discover where the hole went.

He climbed out of the hole to get a lantern. When he climbed back down, he was amazed at what he saw.

Giant slabs of rock seemed to grow everywhere! Some grew from the ground up towards the ceiling. These are called stalagmites. Others grew from the ceiling down towards the ground. These are called stalactites. Jim also saw caverns where water dripped slowly from the ceiling. The water made plopping sounds as it hit the stalagmites.

Jim tried to convince people to come down into the caverns with him. He wanted to show them the wonderful things he had seen. But no one would come. They were scared of the dark and of the bats. They told Jim to stop going into the caverns or he might get hurt.

One day he did get hurt. Jim was exploring deep in the caverns To do this he had to take a lantern so he could see. He also took a long rope so that he would be able to find his way out of the caverns. He was so amazed by the stalagmites and stalactities that he forgot to watch his lantern. The lantern ran out of fuel, and suddenly Jim was plunged into total darkness.

Instead of staying calm, Jim screamed and ran. Since he couldn't see anything, he ran straight into a stalagmite and knocked himself out. When he woke up, his head hurt and he still couldn't see. But he began to crawl around on his knees, searching for his rope. If he could find his rope, he would be able to follow it out of the caverns.

It takes a lot of courage to crawl around in the dark. Jim didn't know what he was touching. He didn't know if there was a hole in front of him, or if something might come out and hurt him. But finally he found his rope and climbed out of the caverns.

Jim never forgot his lantern fuel again! He also decided he needed to have someone with him whenever he went exploring in the caverns. In 1915 he convinced a photographer to follow him into the caverns and take pictures. When the photographer showed his pictures to the people of Carlsbad, everyone wanted to see the caverns.

3. Tell students they are going to hear music by an American composer. Write "Copland" (cope-land) on the board and pronounce it for them, then make them repeat his name after you several times.

4. Ask if anyone can identify what part of the United States (North, South, East or West) New Mexico is in. (West) Make sure they understand that New Mexico is a

state in the United States and not part of the country of Mexico.

5. Play the recording and ask students what it makes them think of. Tell them the title (Hoedown) and that it is from a piece called Rodeo. Ask if anyone knows what happens at a rodeo. What kinds of animals are at a rodeo? What kinds of clothes do people wear at a rodeo?

6. Put on the music and lead students in a free-movement activity to include riding bucking brocos, using a lasso to rope a calf, tipping a cowboy hat, doing a hoedown dance. It's great if you have a class set of cowboy hats for this activity. Have them use imaginary ropes and cattle for the activity.

Craft Activity: Make a Cowboy Vest

Copland's Hoedown is from a larger work called Rodeo, which is about the American west. Copland was the first true American composer, and he defined the American style of music by writing music that reminded people of the old west.

Teacher preparation

Cut a brown paper grocery bag so it can be worn as a vest (arm holes in the sides, a neck hole in the bottom and one big cut down the front).

Student directions

1. Decide on a design you want to put on your cowboy vest. Maybe some mountains, or a horse or some cattle. Then decorate your vest with your own special designs.

2. Put your vest on and be a real cowboy or cowgirl to the music!

United States

Name _____
Date _____

The **United States** is a country on the continent of **North America**.

North America has two bodies of water around it. The **Atlantic Ocean** is to the east of North America, and the **Pacific Ocean** is to the west of North America.

On your map, color the Atlantic Ocean with a purple crayon. Then color the Pacific Ocean with a red crayon.

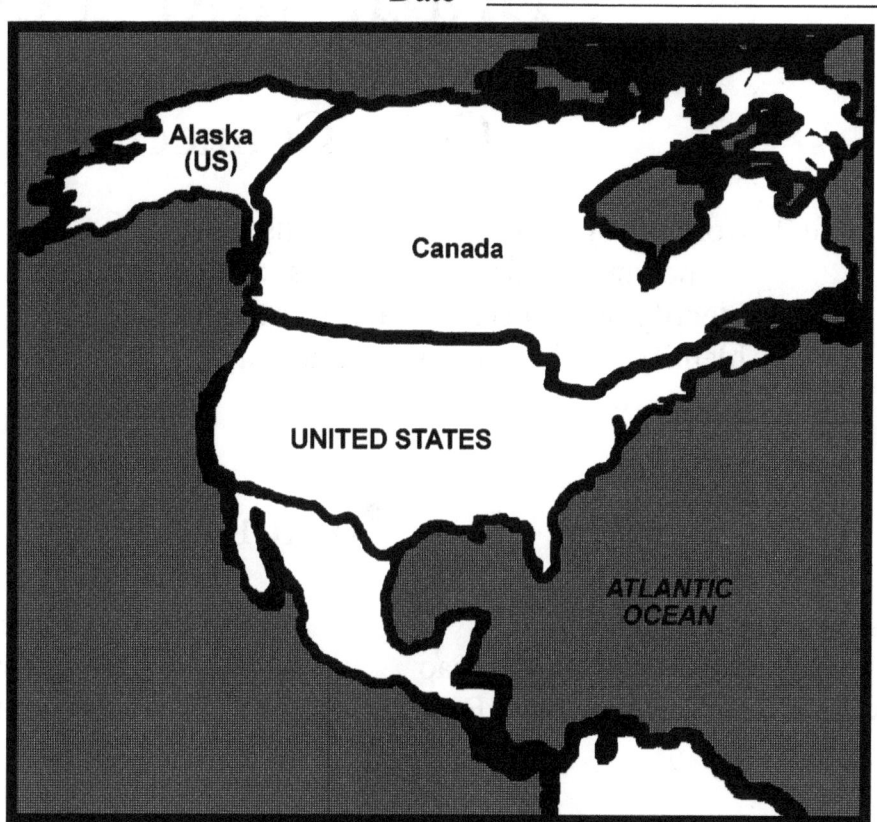

The **Rocky Mountains** are in the western United States. Draw a brown triangle in the western part of the United States to show where the Rocky Mountains are.

The **Appalachian Mountains** are in the eastern United States. Draw a green triangle in the eastern part of the United States to show where the Appalachian Mountains are.

The **Mississippi River** divides the United States down the middle from north to south. It is in the middle of the Rocky Mountains and the Appalachian Mountains. Draw a blue line down the center of the United States to show where the Mississippi River is.

© 2003 Humanics Learning. From *Music Around the World* by Jessica Gates Fredricks

Feijao com Pescao (Beans and Fish) Meia Noite and Alex Acuna Brazil and Peru

Core Connections

Grade 2: World Geography — Spatial Sense
        Name your continent, country and state
        Identify major oceans: Pacific, Atlantic
        Identify continents: South America
        Locate: the Equator

Materials

Movement activity
Recording of Feijao com Pescao
Map of South America and Brazil
Globe

Craft activity
Two different-size plastic tubs
Tape, white paper, glue
Crayons or markers

Procedure

1. Show students a map of South America and Brazil and have them locate the continent and country on a globe.

2. Tell students the following story:

    Once upon a time in the country of Brazil, there was a girl who wanted to be a drummer more than anything else in the world. Her name was Gabriela, but her friends called her Gabi for short. She dreamed of drums at night and thought of drums all day. During the day, she sat in the plaza and watched the musicians play their bongos and congas and cuicas and knew that one day she would play them, too.
    But Gabi's parents were very poor and had no money for expensive things like drums. And even though Gabi knew her parents could never buy her a drum, she could-

n't stop dreaming about a drum of her very own.

One day she said to her mother: "Mama, when will I have a conga drum?"

And Gabi's mother smiled at her daughter, for she knew that Gabi was pretending they were not poor, and said: "Gabrielita, you know your father and I cannot buy you a conga drum — they are the biggest drum of all and very expensive."

Gabi frowned, for she had been speaking aloud as she was dreaming to herself, and said: "Not even a medium-sized drum, like a cuica?"

And Gabi's mother smiled at her daughter, for she knew that Gabi dreamed of being a drummer, and said: "No, Gabrielita, not even a medium-sized drum like the cuica, although I'm sure you would play it very well."

Gabi frowned, for an idea was coming to her as they sometimes do when we are half-awake and half-asleep, and she said: "What about a very tiny drum, like the bongos?"

And Gabi's mother smiled at her daughter, for she saw that Gabi very much wanted a drum of her own so she could play in the plaza with the other musicians, and she said: "Gabrielita, I am certain you will find a way to earn them."

Now Gabi was wide awake and she asked her mother: "Mama, I will catch fresh fish and take them to market — and trade them for bongos!"

And with that Gabi set off for the shores of the Atlantic, which were always teeming with fish, and after she had caught as much as she could carry, she returned to the market and traded her fish for a beautiful pair of bongo drums.

And what do you think she did then?

Why, she sat in with the plaza musicians, of course! They played until the sun went down, and Gabi soon became the most famous bongersero in all of Brazil.

3. On a map of Brazil, have students discover how far Gabi had to walk to get from her city — Rio de Janeiro — to the Atlantic Ocean.

4. Explain the difference between a continent and a country, and have students identify the continent and country in which they live. Then have them identify the continent and country in which Gabi lived.

5. Play the recording of Feijao com Pescao. Have students close their eyes and imagine they are sitting with the plaza musicians.

6. Play the recording again, and this time lead the students in a parade around the room to the beat. Have them imitate your movements at you raise your arms in the air, then put them at your sides, then to the left, then to the right, and repeat this sequence as you march around the room.

Craft Activity: Make a Pair of Bongos

Bongos are two drums of different sizes attached to each other side-by-side. They are hand drums, which means they are played with the hands and not sticks. Students can make a pair of bongos with empty plastic tubs such as the ones used to hold ice cream or butter, or empty cardboard tubs or metal tins if they are available.

Teacher preparation

Every student needs two different size tubs. It helps for students to bring in extras if they have some available. The tubs should be the same height but different diameter for ease of playing.

Student directions

1. If the tubs have tops, remove them before putting the tubs next to each other with the open side down.

2. Tape the tubs together with masking tape. Make sure they are secure!

3. Cover the sides of each tub with white paper and decorate them with crayons.

4. Turn the bongos so that the bottoms of the tubs are facing up. These are your drum heads. Now play the bongos by tapping on the drum heads with your hands.

Brazil

Name _____
Date _____

Brazil is a country on the continent of **South America**. Where do you live?

My country: _____ My state: _____
My continent: _____

On the map below:
    Find the **Pacific Ocean** and color it blue.
    Find the **Atlantic Ocean** and color it green.
    Find the **Equator** and trace it in red.
    Find **Brazil** and trace it in purple.

© 2003 Humanics Learning. From *Music Around the World* by Jessica Gates Fredricks

Finale from New World Symphony
Antonin Dvorak
Czechoslovakia (now the Czech Republic)

Core Connections

Grade 2: Ancient Greece
        Mediterranean Sea, Aegean Sea, Crete, Sparta

Materials

Movement activity
Recording of New World Symphony
Map of Czech Republic and globe

Craft activity
4 paper towel rolls
2 paper plates

Procedure

1. Show students a map of the Czech Republic and have them find the country on a globe.

2. Tell students the following story:

    Once upon a time there was a little boy who wanted to be a hero more than anything in the world. His name was Christopher.
    "Little boys can't do anything by themselves," Christopher wailed. "I can't cross the street by myself, I can't pour milk by myself, and I don't even have my own bedroom. If I was a hero, I could do anything I wanted and no one would stop me."
    Christopher wanted to be a hero so badly that he went around trying to rescue people. He tried to help an elderly woman across the street, but he ended up dropping the packages she gave him. A car ran over the packages and nearly ran over Christopher, but the elderly woman, who turned out to be no so elderly at all, pushed Christopher out of the way at the last second.
    "How can I ever thank you for saving my life?" asked Christopher.

"Next time, try saving someone your own size!" muttered the woman, who picked up her packages and continued on her way, doing quite well without the help of a hero.

So Christopher went off in search of a new person to rescue. Before long he found some people who were very much his own size. It was a group of little girls stuck in a tree. They were precariously perched on a wooden floor in the top of the tree.

Those little girls might fall and get hurt, he thought. I've got to rescue them!

Christopher climbed up the tree as fast a six-year-old hero can. As he pulled himself up the tree, his movements took on a rhythm and he made up a little song.

With one great burst of strength he pulled himself up onto the wooden floor that was perched so precariously in the tree. He beat his chest and sang to the girls:

I'm here to save the day, then he flexed his heroically herculean muscles so the girls could see how strong he was.

Yes, I'm here to save the day, flex, flex, flex.

I'm here to save the day, flex, flex, flex

Yes, I'm here to save the day, flex, flex, flex.

Christopher stopped flexing his muscles — it was hard to tell, because they were really not so heroic or herculean in the first place — and smiled at the girls, sure they would be happy he was here.

But the girls simply giggled. They didn't need a hero — they were playing in their treehouse! And it was a girls-only tree house, so what was this puny pipsqueak doing here in the first place? They didn't need any boy to rescue them — they were girls! But they were clever girls, so instead of yelling at him, they teased him by singing his song like a baby:

You're here to save the day? Why don't you go home?

Oh, you're here to save the day? Why don't you go home?

Christopher couldn't believe what he was hearing — didn't they see that he was a hero? Maybe he hadn't flexed his muscles enough. He tried again:

I'm here to save the day, flex, flex, flex.

Yes, I'm here to save the day! Flex, flex, flex.

But it did not good — the girls started laughing! Christopher's feelings were hurt, but it didn't hurt as bad as when they pushed him! The girls chased him out of the treehouse. Christopher climbed down the tree, thinking he was safe, but the girls kept coming. They chased him out of the yard, down the street, and all the way back to his own house.

And Christopher decided that being a little boy wasn't so bad after all.

3. Tell the students they are going to act out the story. Divide them into boys and girls.

4. Teach each group their part. The boys sing: *I'm here to save the day*, and then flex

their muscles three times to the beat of the music. Repeat this pattern three more times.

5. The girls sing: *You're here to save the day? Why don't you go home?* a total of two times. Tell them to sing as nastily as they can, because they're trying to tease the boys without calling them names.

6. The song sequence is just like the story:
    Boys sing, girls sing, boys sing, girls chase boys

Craft activity: Make a javelin and a discus

The first Olympic games were held in ancient Greece. During the games, the best athletes came from far and wide to see who really was the best. The modern Olympics include events like the javelin and discus. The javelin is a long spear, and the discus is a round, flat, disk. In both events, athletes compete to see who can throw the farthest.

Teacher preparation

Have each student bring in 4 paper towel tubes and 2 paper plates. The paper towel tubes will be taped end-to-end to make a javelin, and the paper plates will be taped together to make a discus. Then hold your own Olympic games to see who is the best in the class.

Student directions

1. Use tape to attach four cardboard tubes end-to-end. This will be your javelin. Make sure the tubes are joined evenly so that the javelin will fly straight through the air.

2. Place two paper plates on top of each other so they look like a flying saucer. There should be empty space between the plates. Then tape them together. This will be your discus. Make sure the plates are perfectly lined up so the discus will fly straight.

Czech Republic

Name _____

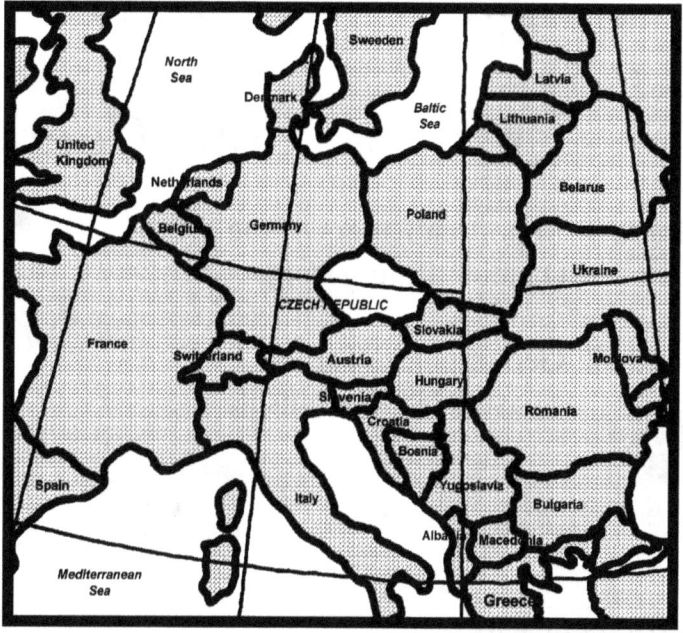

The **Czech Republic** is a country in central Europe. It used to be called **Czechoslovakia**, but in 1992 the country split. Now there are two separate countries, **Slovakia** and the Czech Republic. On your map, color the Czech Republic with a red crayon.

In the southeast corner of the top map, you will find the country of **Greece**.

The lower map is a close-up of ancient Greece. Two bodies of water surround Greece — the **Aegean Sea** and the **Mediterranean Sea**. On the map, color the Mediterranean Sea blue and color the Aegean Sea purple.

There were two great cities in ancient Greece — **Athens** and **Sparta**. Athens was a city-state, and it was in Athens that democracy started. On the map, draw a circle around Athens and draw a square around Sparta.

The island of **Crete** is located in the Mediterranean Sea. On the map, color Crete green.

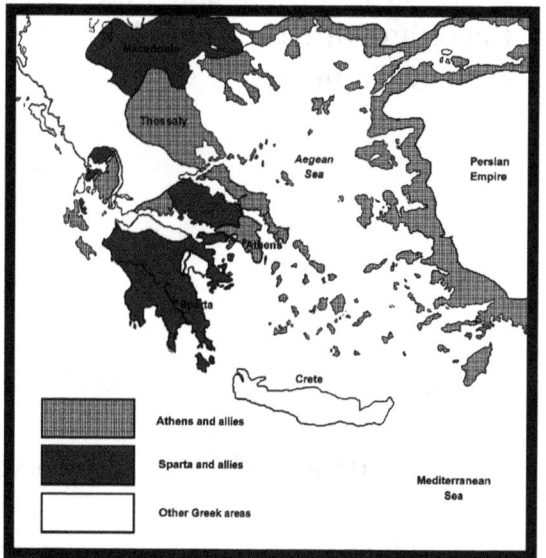

Answer the questions.

1. Two great cities in ancient Greece were _____ and _____.

2. The island of _____ is located in the Mediterranean Sea.

3. Name two bodies of water around Crete: _____ Sea
   _____ Sea

© 2003 Humanics Learning. From *Music Around the World* by Jessica Gates Fredricks

Ride of the Valkyries
Richard Wagner
Germany

Core Connections

Grade 3: Important Rivers of the World
        Danube, Rhine, Volga

Grade 2: Geographical Terms
        coast, island, peninsula

Materials

Movement activity
Pieces of cloth to use as magic capes
Recording of Ride of the Valkyries
Map of Germany
Globe

Craft activity
Empty cereal box
Brown or gray paper
Masking tape
White paper
Markers or crayons

Procedure

1. Show students a map of Germany, and have them find the country on a globe.

2. Tell students the following story:

    Once upon a time in Germany there were some very bad people called Valkyries (pronounced val-krees). The Valkyries rode magic horses that flew through the air. This was way back in medieval times, before TV or radios or airplanes, so horses that flew were really special.
    The Valkyries were bad because they liked to fly through the air until they saw a small village. Then the Valkyries would swoop down on their magic horses, hacking

with swords and knocking over houses and setting fire to everything they could find. This terrified the villagers, and they would run from the village screaming.

But one day a very brave group of villagers decided they were tired of running away. These brave people began to warn people in other towns about the Valkyries. They found some magic cloth that made them run faster than the wind and made long capes out of the cloth. Then they hid in the trees watching for the terrible Valkyries and made up a song to warn villages that the Valkyries were about to descend upon them.

When they saw the Valkyries, they would sing this song as they ran to warn the villagers: "The horses are coming, the horses are coming, the horses are coming, here they come!" And sometimes the Valkyries would see the brave people, and the brave people would have to hide. But the brave people always sang when they heard the tune.

3. Each student will need a "cape" to do the activity. Ask each student to answer a question (Name the bad guys; what country was Wagner from, etc.) before they choose their cape. I have a box of square-yard pieces of cloth that we use for almost everything!

4. Play the recording of "Ride of the Valkyries", and identify the song tune. Teach the song to the students by singing it once to them and having them sing it back. Then sing it together.

5. Play the recording a second time and lead the students in acting out the story. Make movements appropriate to the music, and take your cues from the piece: when it's loud, stand up and flap the cape while singing; when it's soft, get low to the ground and pretend to be hiding from the Valkyries.

Craft Activity: Make a Shield and Coat of Arms

A country's coat of arms is very significant. It can represent honor, loyalty, history, or any number of things. In ancient times, the coat of arms on a knight's shield told what country they fought for. Some shields were made of wood and others were made of metal.

The German coat of arms is made from an eagle emblem. The eagle emblem was first introduced to the Germans by the ancient Romans.

You can make your own shield using an empty cereal box, paper, and some masking tape. Then you can design your own coat of arms and display it on your shield.

Teacher preparation

Have students bring in an empty cereal box. Tape the sides of the box shut so that it can't be opened. Then cut a hole in the back of the box for a handhold.

Student directions

1. Cover the front and sides of your cereal box with colored paper. Use black or gray paper for a metal shield, and brown paper for a wooden shield. Make sure to leave the back of your shield uncovered so you can reach the handhold.

2. Design your own coat of arms on a sheet of white paper. Choose something that is important to you, such as a favorite sport, school subject or animal. Use your favorite colors to color your coat of arms.

3. Carefully glue your coat of arms to the front of your shield.

4. Do the movement activity again, and this time pretend you are a knight with a magic shield instead of a magic cape.

Germany

Name _____
Date _____

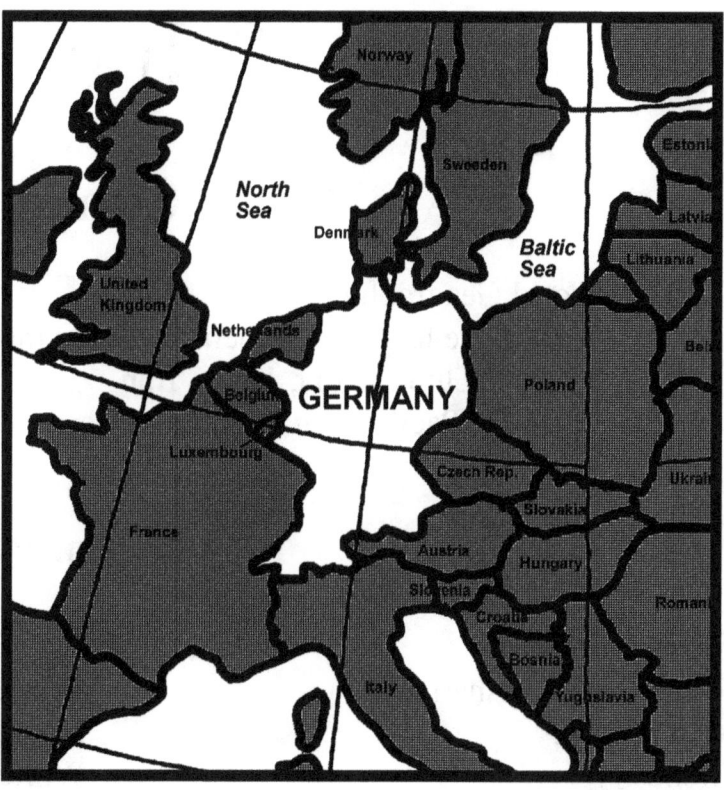

EUROPE

Germany is a country in Europe. It is surrounded by many countries, including Denmark.

Denmark is north of Germany, and is surrounded on three sides by water. Land with water on three sides is called a **peninsula**. Draw a circle around Denmark on the map.

The United Kingdom is west of Germany, and is surrounded on all sides by water. Land with water on all sides is called an island. Draw a triangle around the United Kingdom on the map.

Germany has a short coastline on the North Sea and the Baltic Sea. A coast is land along the water. Color the coast of Germany green.

Rivers are a very important source of water for many Germans. The **Rhine River** is in the west part of Germany. Draw a blue line to show the Rhine River.

The **Danube River** is in the south part of Germany. Draw a red line to show the Danube River.

Another river that is very important to Europe is the **Volga River**. You can't see the Volga River on your map, because it is located in Russia. Russia is east of Germany. Draw an arrow that points to what direction Russia is in.

Answer the questions.

1. Germany is on the continent of _____.

2. Germany has a short coastline on the _____ Sea and the _____ Sea.

3. The Rhine River is in the _____ part of Germany.

4. The Danube River is in the _____ part of Germany.

5. You can't see the _____ River on your map because it's in Russia.

© 2003 Humanics Learning. From *Music Around the World* by Jessica Gates Fredricks

Afshari
Kamil Alipour
Iran

Core Connections

Grade 2: World Geography — Asia
    Asia is the largest continent, with the most populous countries
    Locate: China, India, Japan, Iran
    Identify: Pacific Ocean, Indian Ocean, Arctic Ocean

Materials

Movement activity
Recording of Afshari
Map of Asia
Globe

Craft activity
Small plastic butter tub with lid
Larger cardboard popcorn tub with lid
White paper, crayons, glue
Scissors

Procedure

1. Show students a map of Asia and have them find the continent on a globe. Allow students to discover the large size of China in relation to India, Iran and Japan on a globe.

2. Tell students the following story:

    Once there was a boy who wanted to fly. He sat on a rock overlooking a high cliff, with his tiny legs hanging over the side, listening to the wind blow and dreaming that someday he would be able to fly.
    This boy was not stupid — he knew that people could not fly, and had no intention of jumping off the cliff to see if by some magic he would rise instead of fall — no, this boy knew that the only way to fly was to become one with the wind.

Now you may say this is silly, but in some countries they believe that who you are is a state of mind, not a state of matter. They believe your body is just that — a body — and who you are has nothing to do with that body. So if you believe you are wind, then you will become the wind.

This boy wanted to believe he was the wind more than anything else in the world. He knew that if he could truly believe, then he would rise up off the rock and fly forever.

So the boy spent most of his time sitting on the rock, listening to the wind blow and trying desperately to believe that he was the wind. Day after day he sat, and day after day nothing happened. He did not rise from the rock, no matter how tightly he closed his eyes and imagined himself flying through the air. Without fail, every time he opened his eyes, he was still sitting on the rock.

After several months, the boy became bored of just sitting on the rock — for it was not very much fun to sit for hours without moving — and so he began to bring a set of tablas (tah-blahs) from his house. *Tablas* are small drums of different sizes that are played with the fingertips. The boy sat on the rock and played his tablas. The rhythm was mellow and soothing, and soon the boy found himself closing his eyes. After a time the boy heard the cries of birds coming closer. He kept playing his tabla drums, but he played softer so the birds wouldn't notice him.

The birds stayed for a time, circling him, but the cries soon went away.

Keeping his eyes closed — for that was the proper thing to do when one sat on a rock and played the tabla drums — the boy continued to play. His rhythm sped up and soon he again heard the cries of the birds coming closer. He kept playing his tabla drums, as before, but again he played softer, thinking the sound would scare the birds away.

Again, the birds stayed for a time, circling him, but the cries soon went away.

Now the boy was too curious to keep his eyes closed — even if it was the proper thing to do when one sat on a rock and played the tabla drums — and so he opened them.

And couldn't believe his eyes.

He was flying!

The boy's body had risen from the rock and he was floating — legs crossed, with the tabla drums nestled between his knees — among the birds in the tree tops. In his excitement at flying, the boy's playing became softer, and he drifted back down to the rock. He played louder, and rose slowly into the air.

And that is how the boy achieved his dream and was able to fly.

3. Play the recording and ask students to close their eyes and imagine the story they have just heard as you describe what is happening according to the cue chart below.

4. Divide students into two groups: birds and boys. Have the boys sit on the ground in a circle with their tabla drums (from the craft activity) and the birds against the wall. Make sure to leave space for the birds to flap around the circle.

5. Go through the recording a second time, with students acting out their parts under your direction. Then have students switch parts so everyone gets a chance to be each part.

:00	Boy plays tablas with eyes open
:17	Boy plays tablas with eyes closed
:29	Birds flap around his head; boy plays softly
:51	Boy plays tablas louder; birds rest
1:27	Birds flap around his head; boy plays softly
1:58	Boy opens eyes, sees birds
2:21	Boy and birds fly together, playing and flapping

Craft Activity: Make a Set of Tablas

Tablas are hand drums from India. The set is made up of a two different-sized drums — one made of wood with an animal-skin head and another made of metal with an animal-skin or synthetic head. The drums are typically played with the fingertips.

Teacher preparation

Have students bring in two tubs of different sizes — small butter tubs or cardboard popcorn tubs are good, or even potato crisp containers. Anything round with a lid.

Student directions

1. Cover the sides of each tub with white paper and decorate them with crayons.

2. Put the lids on each tub and play them with your fingertips during the activity.

Asia

Name _____
Date _____

Asia is the largest continent on the globe. It also has the most populous countries, or the countries with the most people in them.

On the map below:
        Find **China** and color it red
        Find **India** and color it orange
        Find **Japan** and color it brown
        Find **Iran** and color it yellow
        Find the **Arctic Ocean** and color it green
        Find the **Pacific Ocean** and color it blue
        Find the **Indian Ocean** and color it purple

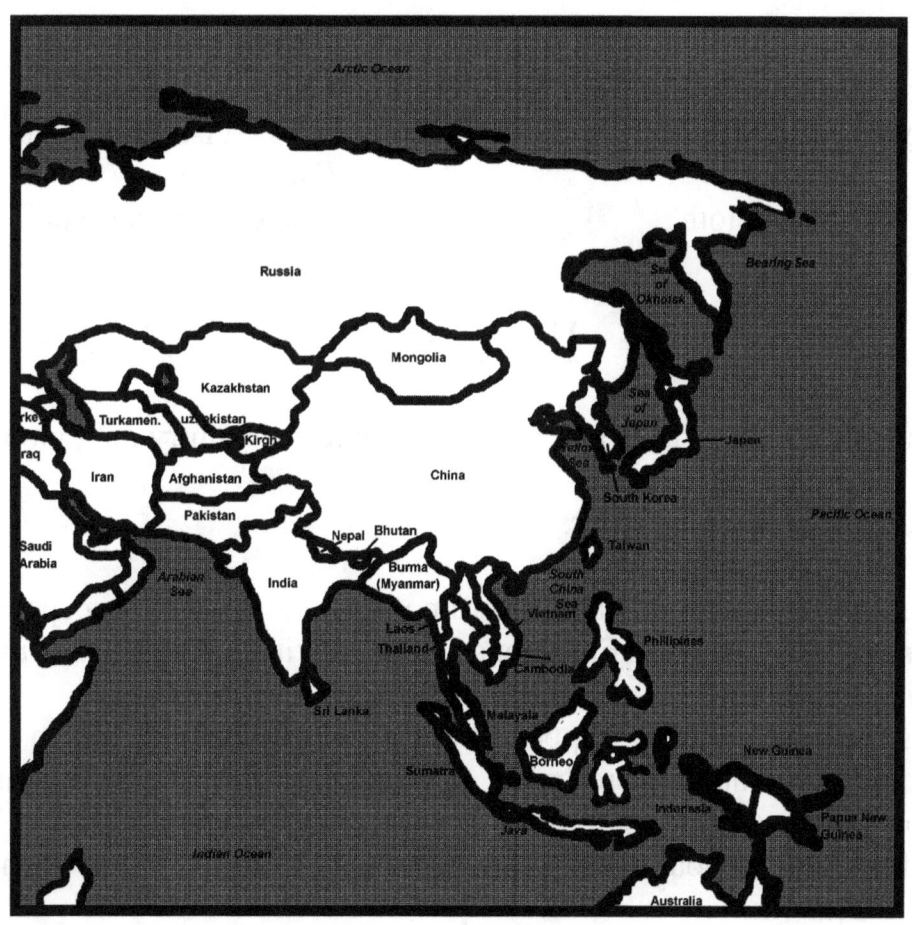

© 2003 Humanics Learning. From *Music Around the World* by Jessica Gates Fredricks

Spring from The Four Seasons Antonio Vivaldi Italy

Core Connections

Grade 2: Science — Insects
Distinguishing characteristics
Six legs and three body parts; head, thorax, abdomen
Most but not all insects have wings

Materials

Movement activity
Recording of Spring from The Four Seasons
Map of Italy
Globe
Square-yard pieces of cloth

Craft activity
Construction paper
Glue, scissors and yarn
Paper plate
Crayons or markers

Procedure

1. Show students a map of Italy and have them find the country on a globe.

2. Tell students the following story:

   In the remote jungles of Italy, it is rumored that the last living species of gigantic killer butterflies still exists. Enormous creatures with a wingspan of up to six feet, the butterflies are omnivores — they eat both plants and animals.
   How could such a thing happen? Funny that you should ask. In the spring of 1964, a group of scientists were trying to develop a cure for Temporary Selective Amnesia, or TSA, a disease that strikes up to 1 billion students daily. The disease strikes suddenly and without warning and can be a deadly inhibitor when it comes to completing homework.

The scientists believed that the secret to curing TSA lie in a special enzyme from a rare plant that could only be found in northern Italy. They began their march into the forest and saw amazing sights: trees that seemed to grow right into the sky, mosquitos larger than a man's hand, and all manner of exotic plants and animals.

Well, a year passed and no one had heard from the scientists. Their relatives became worried and contacted the police in Italy, but no one knew what had happened to them. Then about five years ago, there were some major floods in the region where the scientists disappeared. The water washed all kinds of things into the streets of Italy.

Some of the things were bones, picked clean and bleached white from the sun. There were also scientific instruments, notebooks, and a tape recorder. The notebooks and tape recorder were encased in water-proof containers.

When officials from InterPol listened to the tape, they heard music and several men talking. The men were discussing what a wonderful find they had made, some new plant that was going to cure all diseases. The notebooks described large, man-eating butterflies and there were pencil drawings of the creatures inside the notebooks.

Reading further, the officials discovered the men were the scientists who had gone searching for the TSA cure 25 years ago — the missing scientists were at last found!

But what had happened? The InterPol officials refused to believe that some gigantic butterfly had attacked the scientists — that was ridiculous!

Still, some of the bones had deep gouges in them, as if something enormous had chewed on them. The officials immediately sent out another group to retrace the scientists' steps.

This new group was made up of hunters. Each hunter carried a radio and was told to describe everything he saw. As the hunters crept deeper into the forest, one man reported that he saw "something enormous, with huge wings". Another man reported that they were being followed by "some kind of animal with long teeth that hums music." All at once, the hunters began to scream, and then there was nothing but static. They never came back.

InterPol sent in two more search parties. Each one disappeared without a trace.

Airplanes flying low over the jungle have reported "very large birds". Hikers in the area tell fantastic stories of flying creatures that seem to have no head or legs — only wings.

The creature — named the Vivaldi butterfly — is rumored to fly into remote villages late at night, searching for stray cattle to take back to the jungle.

To this day, many scientists and hunters have gone in search of the fearsome Vivaldi, but none have returned.

3. Divide the students into two groups: scientists and killer butterflies. Tell the scientists to pretend that they have butterfly nets in their hands, and give the butterflies

pieces of cloth to use as wings. Then run through the piece and cue each group as listed. (When one group is moving, the other remains still.) After the first run-through, have the students switch parts so everyone gets a chance to be each character.

Time	Action
:00	Scientists marching through the forest
:31	Scientists swing nets
1:05	Scientists marching
1:13	Scientists swing nets
1:44	Butterflies come out and scientists hide
1:52	Butterflies flutter wings fast
2:11	Butterflies imitate the scientists marching
2:20	Butterflies fly around
2:36	Butterflies fly in a circle
3:03	Butterflies fly away
3:11	Scientists march away

Craft Activity: Make a Butterfly Mask

Students can make a butterfly mask to use during the activity.

Teacher preparation

Punch holes in the paper plate so that yarn can be threaded through for their masks.

Student directions

1. Draw and color a large butterfly on the paper plate and cut it out with scissors.

2. Get your teacher to help you wear the mask by threading the holes with yarn.

Insects

Name _____
Date _____

Insects have six legs and three body parts. Each body part has a name:

      Head   **Thorax**   **Abdomen**

You are going to draw an insect in the space above.
1. Draw a small circle around the word "Head".
2. Draw a medium-sized circle around the word "Thorax".
3. Draw a large circle around the word "Abdomen".
4. Draw two eyes on the the circle that says "Head".
5. Draw six legs coming out of the circle that says "Thorax".
6. Now color your insect!

Most insects have wings, but not all of them. All insects do have six legs. Answer the questions by writing yes or no.

7. A tiger has four legs. Is it an insect? _____

8. A whale has no legs. Is it an insect? _____

9. A bird has wings, but only two legs. Is it an insect? _____

10. An ant has no wings, but it has six legs. Is it an insect? _____

© 2003 Humanics Learning. From *Music Around the World* by Jessica Gates Fredricks

Shake
Tetsuro Naito
Japan

Core Connections

Grade 2: Modern Civilization and Culture — Japan
      A country made up of islands; four major islands
      "Land of the rising sun"
      Pacific Ocean, Sea of Japan
      Mount Fuji, Tokyo
      Japanese flag

Materials

Movement activity
Recording of Shake
Map of Japan
Globe

Craft activity
Construction paper: white and red
Tape, glue, scissors
Four new pencils

Procedure

1. Show students a map of Japan and have them find the country on a globe.

2. Tell students the following story:

    On the island of Japan there was a young boy named Motofumi. His friends called him Moto for short, because Motofumi is a very long name for such a small boy.
    Moto lived near Mount Fuji, which was the tallest mountain in all of Japan, and Moto knew that someday he would climb to the very top of Mount Fuji. He did not know when this wonderful day would come, so he made it a point to ask his mother every morning: "Mother, is today the day I climb Mount Fuji?"
    And every day his mother would answer: "Not today, my little Motofumi."

Soon Moto began to wonder if his mother would ever take him to the top of Mount Fuji. But as he gazed at the mountain day by day, he began to realize just how enormous this mountain was!

And Moto said to himself:: "I will never climb to the top of Mount Fuji as long as I have the strength of a little boy. I must make myself strong like a man."

But how to make himself strong? Moto sat by the mountain and thought. He thought and thought and thought some more and then he saw a bird flying through the air. It was not unusual to see a bird flying through the air, but this bird had a snake clasped tightly in his talons. The snake was wriggling a great deal, and Moto could see how difficult it made flying for the bird.

But the bird kept flying.

"That bird is very strong, for he can lift his own weight plus the weight of the snake," Moto said to himself. "That is how I will earn the strength of a man — by carrying more than my own weight."

So Moto began collecting rocks at the foot of the mountain. At first he lifted stones that were the size of his fist, but eventually he moved on to stones the size of small rabbits and soon he was lifting stones the size of large foxes.

Once he had a good-sized pile, Moto began running with the stones. The little ones at first, and then the medium-sized stones and finally the large stones.

At first it was difficult to run with even the small stones, but after several years Moto had earned the strength of a man and he did indeed climb Mount Fuji.

3. Play the recording and tell students that they are going to learn Moto's special strength exercises. Have them listen as you describe what they will be doing by following the cue chart below.

4. Play the recording a second time and invite students to follow your lead as you direct them through Moto's special strength exercises.

    :00   Moto bounces on tip toes
    :22   Moto does deep knee bends to bass beat
    :40   Moto stretches arms (up, side, side, down, then reverse)
    1:07 Moto jogs in place
    1:27 Moto bounces on tip toes
    1:37 Moto plays drum beat on his chest
    2:14 Moto jogs in place
    2:44 Moto stretches arms
    3:01 Moto does deep knee bends to bass thump
    3:14 Moto practices kicks
    3:28 Moto falls to ground, exhausted

Craft Activity: Make a Japanese Flag Pencil Topper

Students can make a Japanese flag to top their pencils.

Teacher preparation

Have each student bring four new pencils for this activity. Before students arrive, cut pieces of construction paper (red and white) in half and give students one of each.

Student directions

1. Fold the white paper in half, and then fold it in half again.

2. Now open the white paper and cut along the creases so you have four equal-sized rectangles of white paper.

3. Fold the red paper in half, and then fold it in half again.

4. Now trace a milk cap-sized circle onto the folded red paper. Cut out the circle — do not open the red paper before you cut out the circle! You should have four red circles when you are done cutting.

5. Glue the red circles into the center of the white rectangles. This is the Japanese flag.

6. Now attach the four flags to your four new pencils by wrapping one end of the white rectangle around the end of your pencil and securing it with tape. Be sure to attach the flags to the pencils away from the eraser!

Japan

Name _____
Date _____

Japan is a country off the coast of **Asia**. Japan is a country made up of islands. There are four major islands: **Hokkaido, Honshu, Kyushu,** and **Shikoku**. It is known as the "Land of the rising sun."

Japan is surrounded by the Pacific Ocean and the Sea of Japan. Its highest mountain is Mount Fuji. The capital of Japan is Tokyo.

Answer the questions
1. How many major islands does Japan have? _____
2. Japan is known as the "Land of the rising _____."
3. Is Japan an island? _____
4. What is the capital of Japan? _____

On the map below:
      Find the **Pacific Ocean** and color it blue
      Find the **Sea of Japan** and color it green
      Find **Tokyo** and draw a box around it with a red crayon
      Find **Mount Fuji** and draw a triangle around it with a brown crayon

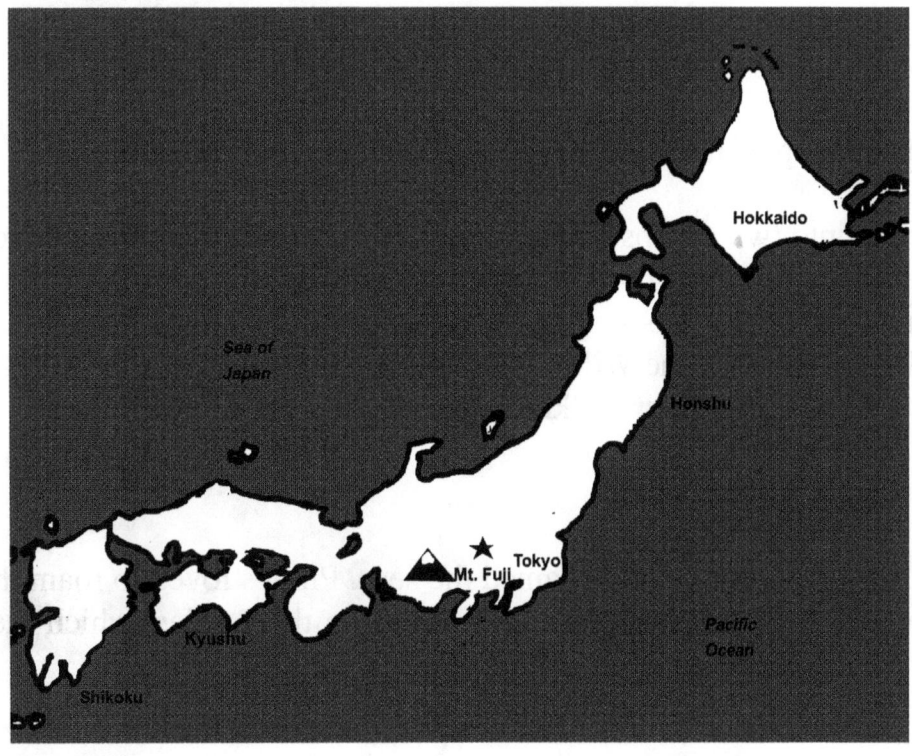

© 2003 Humanics Learning. From *Music Around the World* by Jessica Gates Fredricks

William Tell Overture
Gioacchino Rossini
Italy

Core Connections

Grade 3: World Geography — Geography of the Mediterranean Region
　　　　Red Sea, Aegean Sea, Adriatic Sea, Persian Gulf
　　　　Greece, Italy, Saudi Arabia

Materials

Movement activity
Recording of William Tell Overture
Map of Italy
Globe
Tubes from craft activity

Craft activity
Paper towel tube
Paper plate, glue
Yarn, white paper
Crayons

Procedure

1. Show students a map of Italy and have them find the country on a globe.

2. Divide the class into two groups (pirate ships). It's best if the groups are facing each other while sitting. Tell one group that they are now on the Rossini pirate ship, and any time you talk about the Rossini pirates, you are talking about them. Tell the other group that they are now on the William Tell pirate ship, and any time you talk about the William Tell pirates, you are talking about them.

3. Tell students the following story:

　　　A long time ago fierce pirates roamed the seas. Pirates loved to roam the waters around Italy because it was a peninsula with water on three sides, which meant they could plunder all they wanted.

One day a pirate ship landed on the beach and began to plunder the gold. It was called the Rossini pirate ship. Pirates on the Rossini ship wore black eye patches and liked to growl. Let me hear your pirate growls. (Listen) The Rossini pirates believed that they were the leanest, meanest, roughest, toughest pirates on the sea.

The next day another pirate ship landed on the beach. This ship was called the William Tell pirate ship. Pirates on the William Tell ship wore black face masks and liked to say "aaargh". Let me hear you say "aaargh". (Listen) The William Tell pirates believed that they were the leanest, meanest, roughest, toughest pirates on the sea. And they wanted the gold!

The leader of the William Tell called out to the Rossini ship: "Hey! Hand over that gold!"

And the leader of the Rossini said: "You can't have it because we're the leanest, meanest, roughest, toughest pirates on the sea!" And the Rossini pirates cheered.

But the leader of the William Tell said: "Aaaargh! That can't be — because we're the leanest, meanest, roughest, toughest pirates on the sea!" And his pirates cheered.

The pirates stared at each other. The Rossini pirates growled as softly and meanly as they could (listen) while the William Tell pirates said "aaargh" as softly and meanly as they could (listen).

After much growling and aaarghing, the leader of the Rossini said: "Only the leanest, meanest, roughest, toughest pirates on the sea should get the gold."

And the leader of the William Tell said: "Aaaargh! But how will we decide which ship has the leanest, meanest, roughest, toughest pirates on the sea?"

The leader of the Rossini smiled and said: "We will have a pirate duel. All pirates, all swords and no guns." For everyone knew that no real pirate ever used a gun.

So the Rossini pirates pulled on their fighting pirate eye patches and growled softly to themselves (listen), and the William Tell pirates pulled on their fighting pirate eye masks and said "aaargh" softly to themselves (listen).

3. Play the recording and ask students to imagine the pirates acting out the story as you cue from the form below.

4. Play the recording a second time and have students perform their cues (growls, aaarghs, and stares) without getting out of their seats for the sword fight.

5. Play the recording a third time and have students perform the entire activity — remind them that their sword only touches other swords, not other bodies!

Fanfare (pirates stare at each other)
Rossini ship growls (remain in seat)

William Tell ship aaarghs (remain in seat)
Stare
Rossini ship growls
Loud-soft-loud (loud: yell "sword fight", all students have a sword fight with pirate from other ship. Soft: pirates fight in slow-motion and make no contact with anyone else's sword — we should hear only music. Loud: yell "sword fight", all student clash swords once and then return to seats)
William Tell ship aaarghs (remain in seat)
Stare
Rossini ship growls (remain in seat)
Fight to the death (yell "sword fight" and pirates fight until the end of song)

Craft Activity: Make a Sword and Eye Patch/Face Mask

Students can make a sword and eye patch or face mask to use during the movement activity.

Teacher preparation

Divide students into two pirate ships and tell them what to make: eye patch or face mask.

Student directions

1. Draw an eye patch or face mask on the paper plate and cut it out with scissors.

2. Decorate the patch or mask with crayons.

3. Wear the patch or mask by punching holes in it and then threading the holes with yarn.

4. Cover your paper towel tube with white paper and then draw a handle on one end. This will be your sword.

Pirates on the Sea

Name _____
Date _____

Pirates don't ride in cars. They don't ride in trucks. You wouldn't find a pirate in an airplane, or in the jungle.

Pirates live on the sea. It's very important that they know the different bodies of water around them. If they didn't, they would get lost!

On the map, locate the landmarks and color them in.

Find **Saudi Arabia**. Color it yellow. Find the **Red Sea**. Color it red. Find the **Persian Gulf**. Color it orange.

Find **Greece**.
    Color it pink.
Find the **Aegean Sea**.
    Color it purple.

Find **Italy**.
    Color it brown.
Find the **Adriatic Sea**.
    Color it blue.

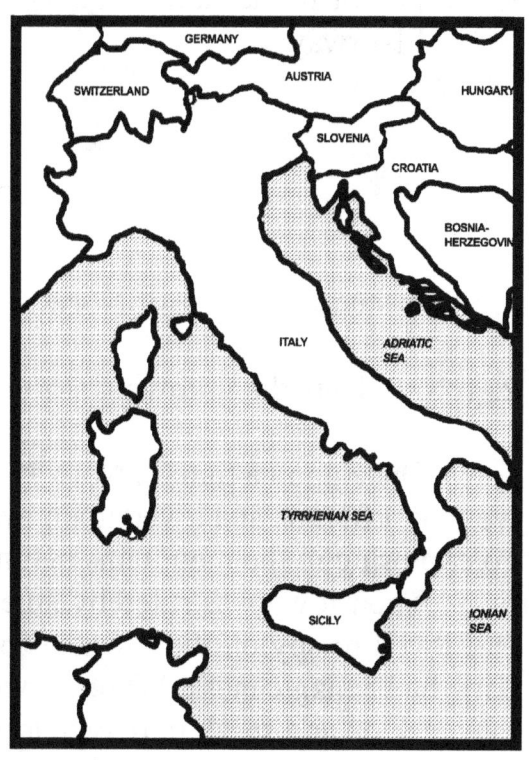

© 2003 Humanics Learning. From *Music Around the World* by Jessica Gates Fredricks

In the Hall of the Mountain King
Edvard Grieg
Norway

Core Connections

Grade 3: The Vikings
       From an area now called Scandinavia (Denmark, Sweden, Norway)
       Northern Hemisphere, Southern Hemisphere, equator
       Also called Norsemen, they were skilled sailors and shipbuilders
       Earliest Europeans to come to North America (Greenland, Canada)

Materials

Movement activity
Black masks
Recording of In the Hall of the Mountain King
Map of Norway
Globe

Craft activity
Paper plates
Rubber bands
Scraps of colored paper
Glue sticks

Procedure

1. Show students a map of Norway and have them find the country on a globe.

2. Tell students the following story:

    Once upon a time in Norway there were two boys named Peter and Eddie. They were best friends and loved to do everything together. What they loved to do most was go exploring in the mountains behind their town.
    Their town was ruled by an evil king. The king lived in a hall in the mountains and loved to spy on the townspeople. Everyone called him the Mountain King. The King had a magic mask. Whoever wore the mask became invisible. The king would put the mask on and sneak into town to find out what people were saying about him. Many

of the townspeople were put into jail because they said something bad about the King when they thought he couldn't hear them.

One night Peter and Eddie crept into the hall of the Mountain King. They snuck past the sleeping guards outside the hall, and past the snoring trolls inside the hall, right into the King's bedroom. They were as silent as they could be, not even making a sound when they breathed. Together they slid the mask out from under the King's pillow and carried it back to the town, where the people threw a party and called both boys heroes.

But in the morning, the King was furious! He called all his trolls to kneel before him. "Bring me the person who stole my mask!" he thundered. "If I don't have the person who stole my mask by tomorrow, I'll throw you all in the dungeon!"

The trolls ran to town as fast as they could and found out what had happened to the King's mask. That night they hid under Peter's bed and waited for him to fall asleep. Then they grabbed him and ran as fast as they could back to the King.

When the King saw it was a boy who stole his mask, he was even madder than before, and ordered that Peter be thrown into the dungeon. Then he asked his trolls to hand over the mask.

The trolls were confused — the King hadn't said to bring back the mask. He'd said bring him the person who stole the mask! The King became furious again and demanded that they bring him the mask or they would be thrown in the dungeon. The trolls shook their heads and wandered off, grumbling. The King could be very difficult sometimes.

What the trolls didn't know was that the mask was hidden under Eddie's pillow. The trolls also didn't know that Eddie had seen them snatch Peter away. And Eddie was very upset. Peter was his best friend and no one was going to lock Eddie's best friend up in a dungeon!

Eddie waited until everyone in town was asleep. He put on the mask and crept out of the village and into the forest until he came to the hall of the Mountain King. He crept past the sleeping guards outside the hall, and past the snoring trolls inside the hall. Eddie snuck silently down the stairs into the dungeon, where a guard was sleeping by Peter's cell. Eddie could see the keys on the guard's belt. He very slowly reached out to grasp the keys, then very slowly pulled them off the guard's belt. He took one step towards Peter's cell, then another. Very slowly, he put the key in the lock and began to turn.

Suddenly the lock popped open with a loud *click*! The noise startled the guard, who fell off his chair, knocking the cell door open. The cell door swung wide, knocking the magic mask off Eddie's face. With the mask gone, Eddie was visible and the guard yelled for help.

The boys began to run. They ran up the stairs out of the dungeon. They ran past the trolls who were no longer snoring inside the hall and past the guards who were no longer sleeping outside the hall. They ran all the way back to the town.

    The King woke up to find his mask back under his pillow, and he figured that he had dreamed the whole thing.

3. Each student will need a mask to do the activity. Have each student answer a question (what country was Grieg from, etc.) before they get a "magic" mask.

4. Play the recording and ask students to raise their hands if they think they're hearing the boys escaping from the dungeon (loud and fast) or Eddie sneaking quietly in to rescue Peter (soft and slow). [The piece starts out slow and gets faster. There is a big cymbal crash right when it gets loud — use this as the click when the lock turns.]

5. Discuss slow and soft movements as compared to fast and loud movements. Have a few students demonstrate, then lead students in acting out the story to the music.

Craft Activity: Make a Mask

Students will make a mask to use during the movement activity.

Teacher preparation

Cut large eye holes and a mouth hole in a paper plate for each student. Punch holes in the side of the paper plate, then thread the holes with rubber bands to make a strap for the mask. A chain of four to six medium-sized rubber bands should do the trick.

Student directions

1. Imagine what a magic mask might look like. Then use a glue stick to attach scraps of colored paper to your mask. Be sure to leave the eye holes and mouth hole open.

2. Do the movement activity again wearing your very own magic mask!

Norway

Name _____
Date _____

    Norway is a country in Europe. It is in an area now called **Scandinavia**.

    Scandinavia is located in the **Northern Hemisphere**. If you look at a globe, you will see a line called the equator going around the middle of the Earth. The part of Earth above the equator is called the Northern Hemisphere. The part of the Earth below the equator is called the **Southern Hemisphere**.

    Scandinavia includes two other countries: **Denmark** and **Sweden**.

    On the map, draw a circle around Denmark. Then draw a circle around Sweden.

    The **Vikings** were a group of people who lived in Scandinavia during ancient times. Also called **Norsemen**, they were skilled sailors and shipbuilders. They are the first Europeans we know of to come to North America. Look on a globe and find the continent of North America. Then find **Greenland, Canada**, and **Newfoundland**. These are places the Vikings visited long before Christopher Columbus made his famous voyage in 1492.

Answer the questions.

1. Norway, Sweden, and Denmark used to be known as _____.

2. Scandinavia is located in the _____ Hemisphere.

3. The Southern Hemisphere is the part of the Earth below the _____.

4. The Vikings were also called _____.

5. Norsemen were skilled _____ and _____.

© 2003 Humanics Learning. From *Music Around the World* by Jessica Gates Fredricks

Samuel Goldenberg and Schmuyle from Pictures at an Exhibition
Modeste Mussorgsky
Russia

Core Connections

Grade 3: Math — Money
    Write amounts of money using dollar and cent signs
    Make change, using as few coins as possible

Materials

Movement activity
Recording of Pictures at an Exhibition
Map of Russia
Globe

Craft activity
Glue or tape
Construction paper
Crayons or markers
Unlined white paper

Procedure

1. Show students a map of Russia and have them find the country on a globe.

2. Tell students the following story:

    This is a story about two men who lived in the same village. One man was not too old and not too young. He was very tall and had a very low voice. His voice was so low it sounded like a train rumbling by when he spoke. And when he laughed it sounded like thunder. His name was Goldenberg.
    Goldenberg was a very rich man. He was so rich that he didn't have to go to

work at all — he had other people working for him. Every day when people passed by his house — which was very big and very expensive and in a very rich part of town — they all wanted to be like Goldenberg.

In a very poor part of the village lived another man named Schmuyle. Schmuyle was so poor that he didn't even have a house to live in. He lived on the street and did odd jobs for people.

One day Schmuyle came to the part of town where the houses were all very big and very expensive. Schmuyle was very very hungry because he hadn't eaten in several days. He saw that Goldenberg's windows needed washing. The windows were very dirty and covered with dust.

Schmuyle knocked on the door of Goldenberg's house and asked to speak with the man of the house.

"Who stands at my door?" boomed Goldenberg's deep voice.

"It is Schmuyle," he said in a high voice, "I have come to wash your windows."

"My windows don't need washing — they're clean as a whistle!"

Schmuyle looked at Goldenberg's windows — which were not clean at all — and then at Goldenberg's white shirt — which was very clean indeed — and said: "If your windows are so clean, why don't you rub your shirt against them? If the windows are clean, your shirt will not get dirty."

Now, Goldenberg was a very rich man, and being a rich man, he wanted to wear nice clothes all the time. He walked over to the window, but when he saw how much dirt was there, he changed his mind.

"Mr. Schmuyle," he said — for Goldenberg realized that if he didn't get Schmuyle to clean the windows, people might begin to think he was not a rich man after all — "I would be delighted if you would do me the honor of cleaning my windows today."

"Well now, Mr. Goldenberg," Schmuyle said — for Schmuyle realized that Goldenberg wanted him to clean the windows and was willing to pay him well for the work — "I would be delighted to clean your windows but I don't have anything to clean them with."

So Goldenberg gave him some money to buy cleaning rags and sent Schmuyle to the store.

When Schmuyle returned, he said, "Mr. Goldenberg, I would love to clean your windows but I don't have a bucket to put the water in."

So Goldenberg gave him some money to buy a bucket and sent Schmuyle to the store.

When Schmuyle returned, he said. "Mr. Goldenberg, I really want to clean your windows but I don't have any soap to put in the bucket."

So Goldenberg gave him some money to buy some soap and sent Schmuyle to the store.

When Schmuyle returned, he cleaned the windows and invited Goldenberg to inspect his work. Goldenberg was impressed.

"Thank you for doing such an excellent job on my windows," said Goldenberg as he pulled out his wallet to pay Schmuyle. "Here's the $20 I promised you, plus $5 for working so fast."

With that, Schmuyle tipped his hat to Mr. Goldenberg and went on his way — with new cleaning rags, a bucket, and lots of soap. And do you know that in five years Schmuyle had made enough money to buy his own house?

3. Play the entire recording of Samuel Goldenberg and Schmuyle (it's very short) and ask students if they can guess which voice was Goldenberg's and which was Schmuyle's. (High trumpet — Schmuyle, deep bass — Goldenberg) Review the story and then listen again, identifying when the changes in character voices take place and asking students to imagine the characters acting to the music without any words.

4. Assign students into pairs of Goldenbergs and Schmuyles and allow them to act out the story as you play the recording a third time. Remind students that they have to convince you of their roles without any words or sounds — only facial expressions and movements.

Craft Activity: Make a Wallet

Students can make a wallet that will hold their practice money for the movement activity.

Teacher preparation

Each student needs construction paper, unlined white paper, crayons and glue.

Student directions

1. Fold the construction paper in half long-ways so that it forms a rectangle shape.

2. Now fold the short ends of the rectangle in about one inch and tape them down.

3. Fold the construction paper in half to make a wallet. Use the white paper and crayons to draw dollar bills. Then color them, cut them out and put them in your wallet!

Goldenberg

Name _____
Date _____

Goldenberg was a very rich man. He had lots of money. When you have lots of money, you have to know how to keep track of it. If you don't know how to keep track of your money, you will lose it.

Goldenberg gave Schmuyle twenty dollars for washing his windows. You could say:

twenty dollars   = $20

What if Goldenberg gave Schmuyle more money? Write the money Goldenberg gives Schmuyle in numbers — remember to use the dollar sign!

fifty dollars   =   _____

forty dollars   =   _____

ten dollars   =   _____

thirteen dollars   =   _____

sixty-two dollars   =   _____

But what if Goldenberg gave Schmuyle less money? Write the money Goldenberg gives Schmuyle in numbers — remember to use the cents sign!

fifty cents   =   _____

ten cents   =   _____

Goldenberg wants to give Schmuyle 12 cents. What is the least amount of coins he can give him? (circle your answer)

2 nickels and 2 pennies   **1 dime and 2 pennies**   **1 quarter**

© 2003 Humanics Learning. From *Music Around the World* by Jessica Gates Fredricks

1812 Overture
Peter Tchaikovsky
Russia

Core Connections

Grade 3: World Geography — Spatial Sense
        Name your continent, country, and state
        Identify major rivers: Ob River, Volga River
        Identify major oceans: Arctic Ocean, Pacific Ocean

Materials

Movement activity
Recording of 1812 Overture
Map of Russia
Globe

Craft activity
Two paper plates
Strips of construction paper
Glue, crayons, scissors

Procedure

1. Show students a map of Russia and have them find the country on a globe. Tell students that they may also find Russia called the U.S.S.R. (Union of Soviet Socialist Republics) on some maps and globes.

2. Tell students the following story:

    Ryan was walking home from school when he heard a tremendous explosion behind the old warehouse. He turned just in time to see smoke and fire pouring out of the side of the building and ran over as fast as he could.
    Behind the warehouse he found a tiny man in a white lab coat. The man was covered in soot and coughing terribly from the smoke. Ryan pulled him to safety.
    "Are you all right?" Ryan asked. The man looked like he was in pain.
    "I'm okay, but the peasants are going to die if you don't help them right now!"

The man coughed again, and as he coughed Ryan saw him wince in pain. Then Ryan saw why — the man's leg was broken!

"I should get a doctor—"

"There isn't time!" the man said. "You have to help the peasants now!"

"Sir, I don't know what you're talking about but your leg looks broken and—"

"Young man, I am a scientist, and I am talking about the Russian peasants. Now are you going to help them or do I have to find someone else?"

Ryan looked at the old man. "What do I have to do?"

"I came here in a time machine. The year is 1812, and the peasants in Russia are fighting for their lives on the front lines of the war."

Ryan frowned. "You can't be serious."

"How do you think I got here?!" The man said, coughing. "A rebel group of Russian peasants are fighting to reclaim their homeland from the French invaders. If you don't go back there this very instant, thousands of people are going to die!"

Ryan ran to the back of the warehouse and stepped inside the time machine.

When he stepped out, a scruffy man ran up to him and handed him a pointed stick. "Here — you'll need this if you're going to help. Follow me to the bell tower — it's our best chance."

Ryan blinked as the man ran off, screaming to the assembled people: "The invaders have a terrible new weapon called a cannon that can tear down buildings," the scruffy man said, "but Dr. Tchaikovsky has sent us someone who will watch for the cannons and warn us!"

The scruffy man pushed Ryan into the bell tower and said: "When you see the cannons, sing out 'I see the cannons moving, there they are' and point in their direction."

And then the man was gone, and 30 peasants stared at Ryan, waiting.

At first cannons were hard to see because they were so far away, but as they got closer Ryan pointed and sang — and his new rebel friends did likewise. Suddenly there was a noise from below — the invaders were trying to break down the door!

Silently, they hid behind the trap door that the scruffy man had shown them. No one made a sound. They saw invaders from cracks in the floor above. They looked very mean!

The bells overhead began to ring — and they were terribly loud! The invaders began stomping on the floor, trying to find the opening to the secret trap door. They held their hands over their ears because the bells were so loud. They were shouting to one another, trying to be heard, but the bells were too loud and hurt their ears. Finally, the invaders left the bell tower.

3. After reading the story, play the recording and ask students to listen for how many times they hear a cannon in the piece. Play the recording a second time and tell stu-

dents what's happening by following the cue chart below.

4. Divide students into invaders (French) and rebels (Russians) and go through the piece a third time with students acting out their parts.

opening horn line: I see the canons moving, there they are (4 times)
variation: I see the cannons (4 times)
horn line: I see the cannons moving there they are (once before the cymbals)
    :44 — cymbal crashes, gets faster (invaders breaking the door down)
    :50 — descending strings, gets slower (rebels hide in trap door)
    1:35 — middle section with church bells/voices (invaders stomp on tower floor — timpani)
invaders: We know you're here, we know that you're hiding here (2 times before cymbal)
    3:03 — I see the cannons moving, there they are (7 times)

Craft Activity: Make a Bell on a Chain

Bells in towers are played by pulling a long chain that runs from the bell to the bottom of the tower. Make bells and hang them all over the classroom!

Teacher preparation

Cut strips of construction paper for students to make paper chains, about 20 per student.

Student directions

1. Make a paper chain by folding one strip of paper into a circle shape and fastening it with glue. This is your first link. Then pass another strip through the first circle and make a new circle. Keep doing this until you have one strip left.

2. Draw a large bell shape on the paper plate and cut it out. Trace that shape onto the other paper plate and cut it out. Decorate the shapes and then glue them together.

3. Attach the bell to the chain using the last strip of paper.

Russia

Name _____
Date _____

Russia is a country on the continent of **Europe** and **Asia**. Where do you live?
My country: _____ My state:_____
My continent: _____

On the map below:
    Find the **Ob River** and trace it with a green crayon.
    Find the **Volga River** and trace it with a red crayon.
    Find the **Arctic Ocean** and color it gray.
    Find the **Pacific Ocean** and color it blue.

© 2003 Humanics Learning. From *Music Around the World* by Jessica Gates Fredricks

Malambo from Estancia
Alberto Ginastera
Argentina

Core Connections

Grade 4: Science — Geologic Time
    Scientists have organized the earth's history into four major eras:
    Precambrian Era
    Paleozoic Era
    Mesozoic Era
    Cenozoic (present) Era

Materials

Movement activity
Recording of Malambo from Estancia
Map of Argentina
Globe

Craft activity
Empty 2-liter bottle
Dirt, rocks, plants
Tape, paper, crayons

Procedure

1. Show students a map of Argentina and have them find the country on a globe.

2. Tell students the following story:

    The Andes mountains run along the western edge of Argentina. Since the Andes is the highest mountain range on the South American continent, there are many regions of the Andes that are as yet unexplored.
    Our story begins with a boy named James. This young man thought he was clever because when his mother told him to wash up for dinner, he pretended not to hear her. Instead, James deliberately wandered off into the thick jungle surrounding the Andes mountains.

You see, James had decided to go exploring. And while there's nothing wrong with exploring, it's always a good idea to let your parents or someone else know where you're going, just in case something happens and you get stuck.

But James wasn't thinking about getting stuck. He was thinking about exploring. He saw a bird with brightly colored wings and decided to follow it up the mountain. But then he saw a giant lizard, and decided to follow it instead.

That was going just fine until the lizard saw James following him — and this was one lizard that did not like to be followed. The lizard hissed at James and began to chase him until James finally climbed up a tree to escape.

Feeling a bit silly now, James decided to head home — he was getting hungry, after all — but on the way he slipped on a muddy hillside and fell into a deep hole. He called for help but there was no one around for miles, and so no one could hear him!

Looking up at the sky, James saw there were different layers of rock behind the mud. The rock was all very smooth so he wouldn't be able to climb it, but there were some plant roots sticking out. One was just above his head. James stood on tiptoe. He could almost reach it . . . .

But not quite.

James jumped, reaching as far up as he could. He touched the root but couldn't grab hold. So James jumped up again, and again, and soon he just liked jumping!

Suddenly the root was in his hand, and James pulled himself up. The root slipped, and James tried to hang on but he couldn't — and he slid back into the hole.

But since jumping was so fun, he kept jumping until he grabbed the root again — and this time he pulled himself all the way out of the hole.

And where do you think he went then?

Straight home, of course! And washed up for supper just as nice as you please!

3. Play the recording of Malambo and have students name some things they think of when they hear the piece. Then play the recording a second time and have students close their eyes as you tell what is happening according to the cue chart below.

4. Play the recording a third time and invite students to get up and act out James's adventures in the Andes mountains.

   :00   James playing in his yard
   :15   James hears mother calling and sneaks away
   :42   James sees a bird and follows it up the mountain
   1:02 James sees a giant lizard and follows it
   1:17 James runs from the giant lizard
   1:31 James stops running to catch his breath
   1:48 James falls down a hole and jumps up and down, trying to escape

2:09 James grabs tree and tries to hold on without falling, but soon falls back into hole
2:16 James jumps up and down, trying to escape hole
2:36 James gets out of hole
2:44 James runs home

Craft Activity: Make a Decorative Planter

Students can make a decorative planter out of an empty 2-liter bottle.

Teacher preparation

Have each student bring in an empty 2-liter bottle that has been thoroughly cleaned. Cut the bottle in half and throw away the tops. Students will use the bottom half for their planter — be sure to poke three holes in the bottom of the plastic for drainage.

Student directions

1. Cover the plastic bottle half with white paper and decorate it with crayons.

2. Fill the bottom of the planter halfway with dirt before choosing a flowering plant that will fit in the planter.

3. Once you have planted the flower, water it. Then place small rocks on top of the soil — these will look nice and help your soil retain its moisture.

Geologic Time

Name _____
Date _____

    The earth is very old — billions of years old. It is so old that scientists have organized the earth's history into four major eras. An era is a large chunk of time.

Precambrian Era
The earliest forms of life appear, such as bacteria and blue-green algae. Later in this era, animals like jellyfish begin to appear.

Paleozoic Era
Vertebrates like fish appear. This is when insects and amphibians develop. Simple plants like mosses and ferns begin to appear.

Mesozoic Era
Also called the age of reptiles. We see dinosaurs, flowering plants, small mammals and birds.

Cenozoic Era
    Also called the present era. We see mammoths, gradual development of modern mammals, birds and other animals, humans, forests, grasslands.

Answer the questions below by circling the correct answer.

1. The Mesozoic Era was known as the age of _____.
   a) moss   b) humans   c) reptiles   d) jellyfish

2. The earliest forms of life appeared during the _____ Era.
   a) Precambrian   b) Paleozoic   c) Mesozoic   d) Cenozoic

3. During the Paleozoic Era, _____ and _____ develop.
   a) humans, moss   b) insects, amphibians   c) moss, insects   d) birds, insects

4. In what Era did mammoths live?
   a) Precambrian   b) Paleozoic   c) Mesozoic   d) Cenozoic

5. Simple plants like mosses and ferns begin to appear during the_____ Era.
   a) Precambrian   b) Paleozoic   c) Mesozoic   d) Cenozoic

6. In what Era do we live today?
   a) Precambrian   b) Paleozoic   c) Mesozoic   d) Cenozoic

7. In what Era did the dinosaurs live?
   a) Precambrian   b) Paleozoic   c) Mesozoic   d) Cenozoic

© 2003 Humanics Learning. From *Music Around the World* by Jessica Gates Fredricks

Andante from the Surprise Symphony
Joseph Haydn
Austria

Core Connections

Grade 4: Geography Related to the development of Western Europe
        Mountains — Alps, Pyrenees
        Rivers — Danube, Rhine, Volga, Oder

Materials

Movement activity
Recording of Surprise Symphony
Map of Austria
Globe

Craft activity
2 empty film canisters
10 paperclips
Small rocks

Procedure

1. Show students a map of Austria and have them find the country on a globe.

2. Tell students the following story:

    Haydn was a very well-known composer when he was alive. You might even call him famous. He was so famous that the king of England invited Haydn to visit his country. Hadyn visited England, and though he enjoyed his visit, he was bothered by one very important thing.
    When people in England went to a music concert, they listened very well to the fast parts. They clapped during the exciting, loud parts. But when the music became slow and soft, the people got tired. Sometimes they even fell asleep! This bothered Haydn because sometimes the English people fell asleep during the slow parts of his

music.

Haydn was a very clever man, and he had a good sense of humor. He figured out a way to wake up the English people who fell asleep.

Inspired by his visit to England, he wrote a piece of music that became known as his Surprise Symphony. It was called this because it started with very slow and soft music. It started out soft and got even softer! Haydn wanted the English people to think it was a slow piece so they would fall asleep. Many of them did just that. Their heads began to nod, and one by one, the audience drifted off to sleep. Then, just as they were about to fall completely asleep, the orchestra exploded with sound! The audience jerked awake, much to Haydn's delight. He knew the audience would fall asleep during the slow parts, so to make sure they heard the entire song, he wrote in a loud surprise to wake them up!

3. Listen to the recording up until the big surprise. Ask students to name adjectives to describe the music. How does the music make them feel? Is this the kind of music you would hear at a rock concert? In church? When you're trying to go to sleep at night?

4. Sing the following words to the tune of Surprise Symphony, and teach them to the class:

> *Haydn wrote a symphony,*
> *Silly surprise symphony*
> *Haydn wrote a symphony,*
> *With a big surprise*
> *Haydn wrote a symphony,*
> *Silly surprise symphony*
> *Haydn wrote a symphony,*
> *With a big surprise (pop!)*

5. Ask students to demonstrate ways of moving around that are soft and slow (tiptoeing, creeping slowly, etc.) Then ask students to demonstrate a way of moving for the loud surprise (a jump, or leap, or stomp foot on the ground). Lead students in moving slowly to the music while singing the words softly. Remember to add the surprise!

Craft Activity: Make Loud Shakers and Soft Shakers

Students can make shakers that produce loud and soft sounds using empty film canisters. Most stores that develop film will give the canisters away for free — just ask! Once students have made both kinds of shakers, have them decide which shaker to use for the soft part of the activity and which shaker to use during the loud part.

Teacher preparation

Have students bring in small rocks or plastic beads to use for the loud shaker, and paperclips to use for the soft shaker. For younger children, it's fun to make this part of a treasure hunt — take them outside to look for things that would make soft sounds, and then look for things that would make loud sounds. The possibilities are endless.

Student directions

1. Open both canisters. Be sure to put the tops in a safe place because you'll need them later.

2. Put small rocks or plastic beads in one canister, then snap the top on. Shake the canister. Does it make a loud or soft sound?

3. Put paperclips in the other canister, then snap the top on. Shake the canister. Does it make a loud or soft sound?

4. Use your shakers to perform the movement activity again.

Austria

Name _____
Date _____

    Austria is a country in central Europe. Find it on the map and color it yellow. On the continent of Europe, there are many important geographical features. Two major mountain ranges are the Alps and the Pyrenees.

    The **Alps** are the largest mountain system in Europe. They extend north from near the Mediterranean Sea in France and form a border between France and italy. They continue eastward through northern Italy, Switzerland, southern Germany and Austria. Draw a green line to show where the Alps are on your map.

    The **Pyrenees** are a mountain chain that forms a natural barrier between France and Spain, extending from the Bay of Biscay to the Mediterranean Sea. Draw a brown line to show where the Pyrenees are on your map.

    Europe is also home to four major rivers.

    The **Volga** is the longest river in Europe. It flows through Russia, from St. Petersburg to the Caspian Sea. Draw a blue line to show where the Volga is on your map.

    The **Danube** is the second-longest river in Europe. It begins in southern Germany, then winds east through Austria and near the borders of the Czech Republic, Hungary, and Romania. Draw a purple line to show where the Danube is on your map.

    The **Rhine** is the most important inland waterway in Europe. It forms a border between Switzerland, Austria, France, and Germany. It then flows through Germany and the Netherlands into the North Sea. Draw a red line to show the Rhine on your map.

    The **Oder**, also called the Odra, begins in the Czech Republic and flows north across Poland to form most of the boundary between Poland and Germany before emptying into the Baltic Sea. Draw an orange line to show the Oder on your map.

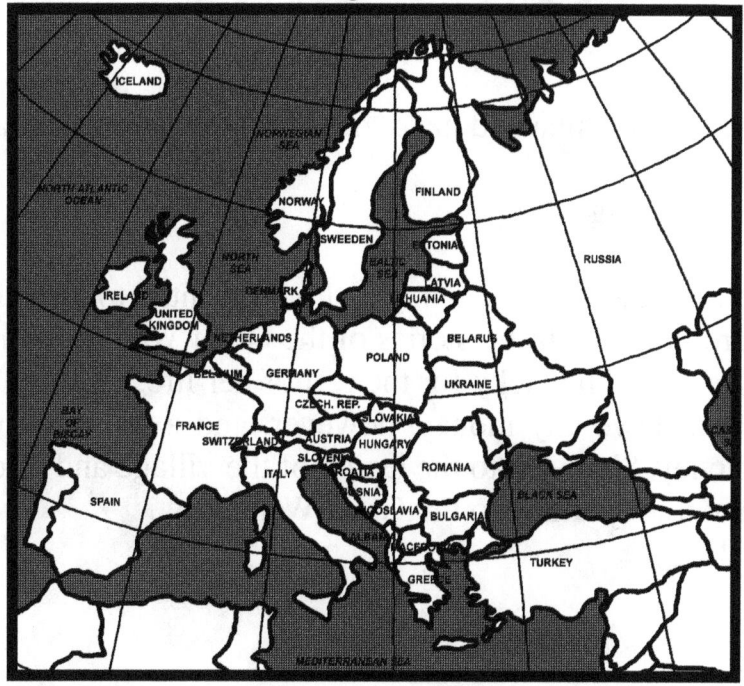

© 2003 Humanics Learning. From *Music Around the World* by Jessica Gates Fredricks

Picking Flowers
Traditional China

Core Connections

Grade 4: China — Dynasties
    Qin Shihuangdi, first emperor, begins construction of Great Wall
    Han dynasty: trade in silk and spices; the Silk Road, invention of paper
    Tang and Song dynasties: highly developed civilization, extensive trade, important inventions (including compass, gunpowder, paper money)

Materials

Movement activity
Recording of Picking Flowers
Map of China
Globe

Craft activity
White paper, crayons
Empty 2-liter bottle
Empty plastic butter tub
Construction paper

Procedure

1. Show students a map of China and have them find the country on a globe.

2. Tell students the following story:

    Once upon a time there was a young girl who wanted to visit the Great Wall of China. She had heard many fantastic stories of the Great Wall and was sure that if she could only see it, she would be lucky for the rest of her life.
    The girl did not have any money, however, and a journey to the Great Wall would take much money. She went to the leader of the village and said: "Oh wise one, how can I get money for a journey to the Great Wall?"

And the wise one said: "The spice merchants have money."
The girl asked: "But how will I get money?"
"You must find something the spice merchants want to buy."
"What do the spice merchants want?"
The wise one smiled. "Spices."
The girl frowned. "Where will I get spices?"
"They grow on the hillsides and have green leaves. They look like flowers."
"Yes, but how will I know which ones are flowers and which ones are spices?"
The wise one smiled. "Trial and error."

So the girl bowed to the wise one and then ran to the hillsides, where she filled her basket with all manner of green leafed-flowers.

When the spice merchants came to market, she held her breath as they sniffed each one of her spices, hoping she had picked the right ones.

"We cannot trade with you," the first merchant said, "because these are not the right kind of spices. We will return in one month." And with that, the merchants left.

So the girl bowed to the spice merchants and then ran to the hillsides, where she filled her basket with different kinds of green leafed-flowers.

When the spice merchants again came to market, she held her breath as they sniffed each one of her spices, hoping she had picked the right ones.

"We will trade with you," the first merchant said, "on one condition."

The merchant smiled at his friends.

"You must agree to bring us more spices — these are of a sort we have not known before, and they are wonderful. We will pay you, of course."

And so the girl not only got her journey to the Great Wall of China, it turned out she was lucky after all, for the spice merchants paid her so well for her spices that she was able to buy a large house and live happily ever after.

3. Play the recording and ask students to close their eyes, imagining the scenes as you call out what's happening according to the cue chart below.

4. Divide students into two groups: girls and spice merchants, and have them act out the story to the music using the props from the craft activity under your direction.

:00   stands, bows, stands, bows
:16   girl kneels to pick leaves
:24   spice merchants come, but will not buy
:38   girl kneels to pick leaves
:46   spice merchants come to trade, find one they like
1:03   girl kneels to pick more of good leaves
1:21   spice merchants come, buy much of the good spice

1:42 girl bows, merchants bow, girl bows, merchants bow

Craft Activity: Make Spice Bottles

Students can make spice bottles to use during the movement activity using an empty 2-liter bottle, white paper, construction paper, scissors, tape and crayons.

Teacher preparation

Each student will need to cut up "spices" from scraps of construction paper. Use a variety of different colors so that each bottle appears to have a mixture of spices. Students will have to cut the paper into very tiny pieces — like confetti — so that it will fit into the neck of the the bottle.

Student directions

1. Cut the construction paper into very tiny pieces. These will be used to represent the spices during the movement activity.

2. Cover the empty 2-liter bottle with white paper and write "Spices" in big letters. Then decorate the bottle with crayons — use lots of red and gold.

3. Use the bottles during the movement activity.

China

Name _____
Date _____

    China is a country on the continent of **Asia**. In ancient times, China was ruled by emperors.
    The first emperor of China was **Qin Shihuangdi**. He ruled from 221 to 210 B.C., and began construction on the **Great Wall** of China. The Great Wall is an enormous structure that stretches 1,500 miles along China's northern border.
    The **Han dynasty** ruled from 206 B.C. to A.D. 220. It is known as the golden age of Chinese philosophy. Beginning in about 100 B.C., a network of trade routes was established to carry goods between Asia and Europe. The earliest, most direct and most used route became known as the Silk Road. It was called the Silk Road because so much of the precious Chinese cloth was traded on it.
    The Han dynasty was known for many things — their trade in silk and spices, the Silk road, and the invention of paper.
    During the **Tang dynasty** (618-907), imperial China reached the height of its wealth and power — it was known as one of the most powerful states in the world at the time.
    The **Song dynasty** ruled from 960 to 1279 and brought China to one of its highest points economically, artistically, and intellectually.
    The Tang and Song dynasties were known for many things — highly developed civilization, extensive trade and important inventions including the compass, gunpowder, and paper money.

Answer the questions.

1. On what continent is China located?
a) Africa   b) Asia   c) Europe   c) Australia

2. Who began construction on the Great Wall of China?
a) Qin Shihuangdi   b) Han dynasty   c) Tang dynasty   d) Song dynasty

3. What two continents were connected by the Silk Road?
a) North America, Asia   b) Africa, Asia   c) Asia, Europe   d) Africa, Europe

4. Which of the following were the Tang and Song dynasties not known for?
a) paper money   b) gunpowder   c) Silk Road   d) invention of compass

5. Which of the following was invented by the Han dynasty?
a) compass   b) paper   c) gunpowder   d) water

© 2003 Humanics Learning. From *Music Around the World* by Jessica Gates Fredricks

Mars from The Planets
Gustav Holst
England

Core Connections

Grade 4: Spatial Sense
        Geography related to the development of Western Europe:
        British Isles, England, Ireland, Scotland, Wales, The English Channel
        Prime Meridian (0 degrees); Greenwich, England

Materials

Movement activity
Recording of The Planets
Map of England
Globe

Craft activity
9 different colors of paper
1 coat hanger
5 feet of string
Scissors

Procedure

1. Show students a map of England and have them find the country on a globe.

2. Tell students the following story:

    Once upon a time there was a young boy named Gus. Gus loved looking at the stars, and he would often sneak out of his window at night to lie in the grass and stare up at the sky. He wanted to be an astronaut and fly through space.
    But Gus had a problem with his heart. He was born with his heart on the wrong side of his chest, and astronauts had to be in perfect health. So instead of being an astronaut, Gus took up the trombone.
    Now, the trombone is a brass instrument that has a very long slide, and Gus liked to imagine that when he was playing his trombone, he was actually commander of a

space ship, shooting down invaders from another planet. Gus had a very active imagination.

Gus grew up and continued playing his trombone, He played all through high school and college, and then became a conductor. A conductor is a person who stands in front of a band and waves his arms to the beat. The conductor keeps the band together.

But Gus never stopped loving space. So he wrote a piece of music for his band to play about space. It was called "The Planets", and it took him five years to write! The piece included the seven planets that Gus loved so much:

> *Mercury, the winged messenger*
> *Venus, the bringer of peace*
> *Mars, the bringer of war*
> *Jupiter, the bringer of jollity*
> *Saturn, the bringer of old age*
> *Uranus, the magician*
> *Neptune, the mystic*

Now, you might be saying: "Wait a minute! Gus forgot one of the planets!" But Gus started writing his music way back in 1914, and when he finished, the planet Pluto hadn't been discovered yet. In fact, Pluto wasn't discovered until 1930, so he had no idea there was another planet out there.

Where were we? Oh yes — The Planets. Gus wrote this piece and included descriptions of each of the planets as he imagined they might look if they were people. He saw the planet Mars as a warrior, creeping through the jungles or sneaking up on some unsuspecting target. He saw the planet Jupiter as a jolly old man, eyes shining brightly and full of laughter.

But what Gus really wanted to know was what you think of his planets. Can you guess which planets you are hearing?

3. Write the names of each planet (ex: Mars, bringer of war) on the board. Tell the students you are going to play some of each planet's song and you want them to guess which planet they are hearing. Play the first minute or so of each song and let them guess until they get it right. Talk about what they are hearing.

4. Tell students they are going to act out Mars, bringer of war. Talk about what kinds of movements soldiers make (ex: creeping slowly, crawling on their bellies, peeking around trees). If possible, talk about trench warfare during World War I. This is a free movement activity — tell students to let the music be their guides. If the music is soft and slow, they should make slow, creeping movements. If the music is loud

and fast, they should make quick movements.

Craft Activity: Make a Hanging Mobile of the Planets

Students can make a mobile of the planets using string, different colored pieces of paper and a coat hanger. Use a different color of paper for each planet (Mercury, Venus, Earth, Mars, Jupiter, Saturn, Uranus, Neptune, Pluto).

Teacher preparation

Have each student bring a coat hanger to school. Cut sheets of colored paper into fourths, enough so that each student gets nine different colors. Each student will need nine pieces of string about six inches long to attach their planets to the coat hanger.

Student directions

1. Draw circles on 9 different colors of paper.

2. Cut the circles out.

3. Write the name of a planet on each circle.

4. Use scissors to punch a small hole in each of the planets.

5. Using a piece of string, tie each planet to the coat hanger in the correct order: Mercury, Venus, Earth, Mars, Jupiter, Saturn, Uranus, Neptune, Pluto.

England

Name _____

England is a country in **Europe**. It is on an island called the **United Kingdom**. On the map, color England yellow.

There are two other countries in the United Kingdom: **Wales** and **Scotland**. Wales is west of England, and Scotland is north of England. Color Wales red, then color Scotland purple.

To the west of the United Kingdom is another island. This is **Ireland**. Color Ireland green.

England is separated from the continent of Europe by a body of water called the **English Channel**. Find the English Channel and color it blue.

A globe is divided into sections by imaginary lines called latitude and longitude lines. Latitude lines go east-west, and longitude lines go north-south. they are numbered by degrees. **The Prime Meridian** is the start of the longitude lines and is found at zero degrees. The Prime Meridian passes through **Greenwich**, England. Find the Prime Meridian on your map and trace it with an orange crayon.

Answer the questions.

1. England is separated from Europe by the _____ Channel.

2. Wales is _____ of England.

3. _____ is north of England.

4. _____ is west of Wales.

5. The _____ _____ is at zero degrees longitude.

6. The Prime Meridian passes through _____, England.

© 2003 Humanics Learning. From *Music Around the World* by Jessica Gates Fredricks

March to the Scaffold from *Symphony Fantastique* Hector Berlioz France

Core Connections

Grade 4: History and Geography
    Locate the region called Normandy in France
    William the Conqueror: Battle of Hastings, 1066

Materials

Movement activity
Recording of March to the Scaffold
Map of France
Globe
Arrow props (see craft activity)

Craft activity
Paper towel tubes
Styrofoam
Masking tape
Paper
Scissors

Procedure

1. Show students a map of France and have them find the country on a globe.

2. Tell students the following story:

    A prisoner in medieval France is scheduled to be executed. He and the other prisoners of the dungeon are placed in foot shackles, put in line and paraded in front of the king's best archers, who jeer at the prisoners and shout insults.
    On this particular day, a prisoner has decided that he does not want to die, not today. During the parade, he waits until the guards aren't looking, then breaks from the parade and throws himself at the king's feet.

"Oh mighty king, thou art so wise and good, and I am so unworthy to grovel at thy feet," says the prisoner, "but I know that your majesty is a gambling man, and I have a wager I believe he might find appealing."

The king, who was very angry that his guards had let one of the prisoners escape, is impressed by the prisoner's boldness. "This is true," says the king, stroking his beard. "Stand up, prisoner, and make your wager."

The prisoner stood. "Your majesty, I submit to you that I am the fastest runner in all the land. I can outrun anything. Even arrows, shot by your majesty's own archers. And I will prove it, if only your majesty will untie my hands and feet."

A crowd had gathered to hear the young man's wager, and the people roared with laughter. "No one can run that fast," shouted a child. "He's a dead man," muttered another.

The prisoner's wager interested the king, but the king was a very clever man. He knew if he untied the prisoner's feet, he would surely run away before the archers could take aim.

"Prisoner, I will untie your hands, but not your feet," said the king. "If you are fast enough to outrun many arrows, then surely you can dodge one arrow with your feet tied. Dodge the arrow, and you will go free."

The prisoner agrees, and the king's best archer takes aim.

3. Tell students that the story has an ending, but you don't know what it is yet. Tell them we have to find out by acting the story out, then divide them into two groups (archers and prisoners).

4. Play the recording and sing it once through for the students, indicating what happens and when. Then teach the parts and have students sit while singing through the action.

Prisoners: I do not want to die today
Archers: We will get you, (then do silent Archer's Dance of Joy)

5. Hand out props. Cheap plastic-and-foam bow and arrow sets can be found at dollar stores, or simply use empty paper towel rolls for mock arrows and have students throw them like spears. Tell students they must listen for your cues during the music — when you form the prisoners into a line, their feet must be "glued" to the floor. The only rule is that when the archers "fire", they cannot move their feet. They can lean, or squat, but their feet must remain on the floor.

6. The song sequence is as follows:
Prisoners march slowly in circle, singing *I do not want to die today*
(archer part always preceded by loud timpani)

Archers sing *We will get you*, then do silent Archer Dance of Joy
Prisoners
Archers
Prisoners: I do not want to die (3 times), form a line facing archers, feet stuck to floor
On signal from teacher (solo clarinet wail) archers make line facing prisoners
Drum roll : teacher calls Ready, Aim, Fire!, and prisoners who aren't hit win.

Craft Activity: Make an Arrow

Students can make an arrow to be used in the movement activity above. Allow them to be creative with their arrows — add fins and nose cones to see which fly the farthest, the straightest, etc.

Teacher preparation

Have each student bring in at least one paper towel tube and a styrofoam cup. Cut 3- or 4-inch diameter circles of paper that can be cut and shaped to make nose cones.

Student directions

1. Make a cut halfway into the paper circle and then wrap it around to make a cone shape. Secure the cone with a piece of tape. This will be the nose cone for your arrow.

2. Use scissors to cut three triangle shapes from the styrofoam cup. These will help your arrow fly straight, so make sure all the triangles are the same size and shape.

3. Use scissors to make three cuts about two-inches long in one end of the tube.

4. Push the styrofoam triangles — called fins — into the cuts on the cardboard tube. Secure the fins with tape to the outside of the cardboard tube.

5. Experiment with your arrow. Throw it to see how it flies without a nose cone, then attach the nose cone with tape and throw it again. See whose arrow flies the farthest!

France

Name _____
Date _____

France is a country in **Europe**. It has coastlines on the Atlantic Ocean and the Mediterranean Sea.

Look on the map and find the United Kingdom. The body of water between the United Kingdom and France is called the **English Channel.**

On your map, color the English Channel with a blue crayon.

Normandy is an area of France that borders the English Channel.

On your map, color Normandy red.

William the Conqueror, also known as the Duke of Normandy, wanted to be the king of England. He claimed the throne of England had been promised to him by his cousin, Edward the Confessor. Edward was king of England from 1042 until 1066.

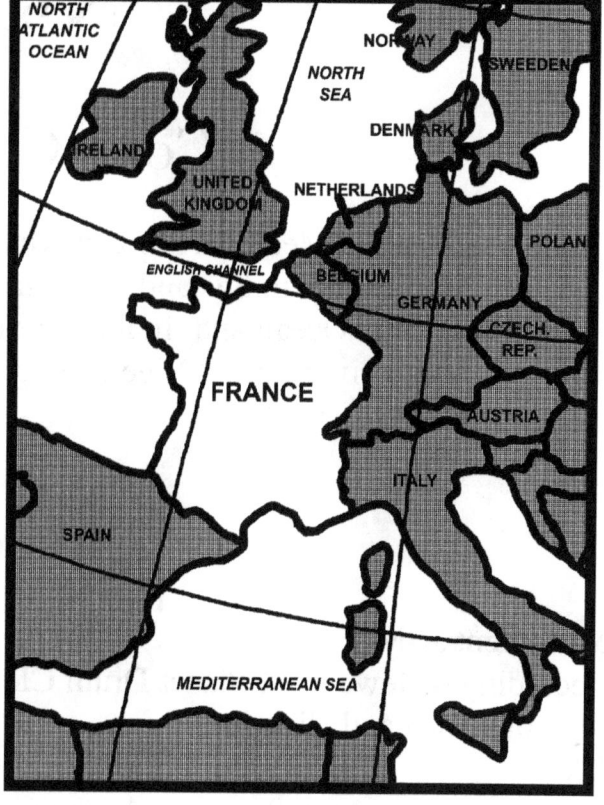

In 1066, William led his fellow Normans to invade England. Led by William, the Normans defeated the English at the **Battle of Hastings**. William then led his forces to London, crushing any resistance he found along the way. On Dec. 25, 1066, he was crowned king of England.

It was after this battle that William became known as the Conqueror. He was the first Norman king of England, and he ruled from 1066 to 1087.

Answer the questions.

1. France is on the continent of _____.

2. _____ the Conqueror was also known as the Duke of Normandy.

3. The Normans defeated the English at the Battle of _____.

4. The Battle of Hastings took place in the year _____.

5. After the Battle of Hastings, William became known as the _____.

© 2003 Humanics Learning. From *Music Around the World* by Jessica Gates Fredricks

Jewe
Babatunde Olatunji
Nigeria

Core Connections

Grade 4: Early and Medieval African Kingdoms — Geography of Africa
           Mediterranean Sea and Red Sea
           Atlantic Ocean and Indian Ocean
           Major rivers: Nile, Niger, Congo
           Madagascar

Materials

Movement activity
Recording of Jewe from Planet Drum CD
Map of Africa and Nigeria
Globe

Craft activity
Two or more paper towel rolls
Construction paper, glue
Crayons or markers

Procedure

1. Show students a map of Africa and Nigeria and have them find both the continent and the country on a globe.

2. Locate which walls in your classroom face north, south, east, and west. Make posters that say each direction and place them on the corresponding wall before reading the following story to students. You will need to divide students into four teams. Each team needs a navigator, a map reader, two recorders, and several musicians. The jobs of each are as follows:

Navigator: tells the team which direction (north, south, east, west) to face in the room
Map reader: reads the map for the team
D-Recorder: records each direction the team takes

L-Recorder: records each location the team visits
Musicians: plays the beat on their chests during the team's journey

3. Tell students that as you read the story, each person on the team must perform their jobs. When you give a direction, each person on the team must face that direction. For example, if you say: "We traveled north to Nigeria", the entire team must face the classroom wall that says north while performing their duties. They will stay this way until you give another direction.

4. Play the recording and tell students that there is only one instrument being used to make all the different sounds. See if they can guess what it is, then tell them it's a person's body. It's a group of several men singing while slapping their chests to produce a variety of sounds and keep a complicated rhythm going all at once.

5. Tell students the following story, being careful not to go on to the next paragraph until each team is ready. Play the recording as you take your journey so that the team musicians have something to play along to on their chests:

   On a hot, dry day in the Kalahari Desert, a team of travelers headed north.
   The team walked north until they arrived at the Congo River. After drinking from the river's cool waters and dozing a bit in the sun, the team walked east.
   The team walked until they reached the shores of the Indian Ocean. They fished in the Ocean until they had had their fill, and then they turned south.
   The team walked this way until they reached a point where they could see the island of Madagascar out in the ocean. The sight was so beautiful that even the musicians stopped playing to stare across the waters. And after they had stared for some time, the team headed north.
   They walked until they reached the Nile River, where again they drank from the river's cool waters and washed their tired feet on the banks of the river. They camped by the river for the night, but when the sun came up they headed west.
   They walked until they reached Nigeria, where they again slept for the night before the sun rose and they continued west.
   They continued until they arrived at the Niger River. At this point they got onto a boat and rode west all the way into Guinea.

6. At this point, tell the students that each team now has to make their own way to the Mediterranean Sea. They must make it to the Mediterranean Sea in four moves or less, using only the four directions posted in the classroom. The recorders, map reader, musicians and navigator must do their job as they complete the task. Let the recording play as students take 15 minutes to complete this task.

Craft Activity: Make an Expedition Telescope

Students can make a telescope to accompany them on their African expedition using two paper towel rolls of slightly different size, construction paper, glue, and crayons.

Teacher preparation

Have each student bring two or more paper towel rolls from home.

Student directions

1. Determine which paper towel roll is slightly smaller than the other and put one inside the other. If yours are the same size, trade with a friend until you find two that fit one-inside-the-other.

2. Cover the outer paper towel roll with construction paper and decorate it with crayons.

3. If possible, cover the inside paper towel roll with a different color of construction paper and decorate it with crayons.

4. Put your telescope together and use it on your African expedition!

Africa

Name _____
Date _____

Africa is a very large continent. It has many different geographical features. Find the landmarks below and identify them on your map.

Color the **Mediterranean Sea** purple
Color the **Red Sea** red
Color the **Atlantic Ocean** yellow
Color the **Indian Ocean** blue
Color the island of **Madagascar** brown
Trace the **Nile River** with a red crayon
Trace the **Niger River** with a purple crayon
Trace the **Congo River** with a green crayon

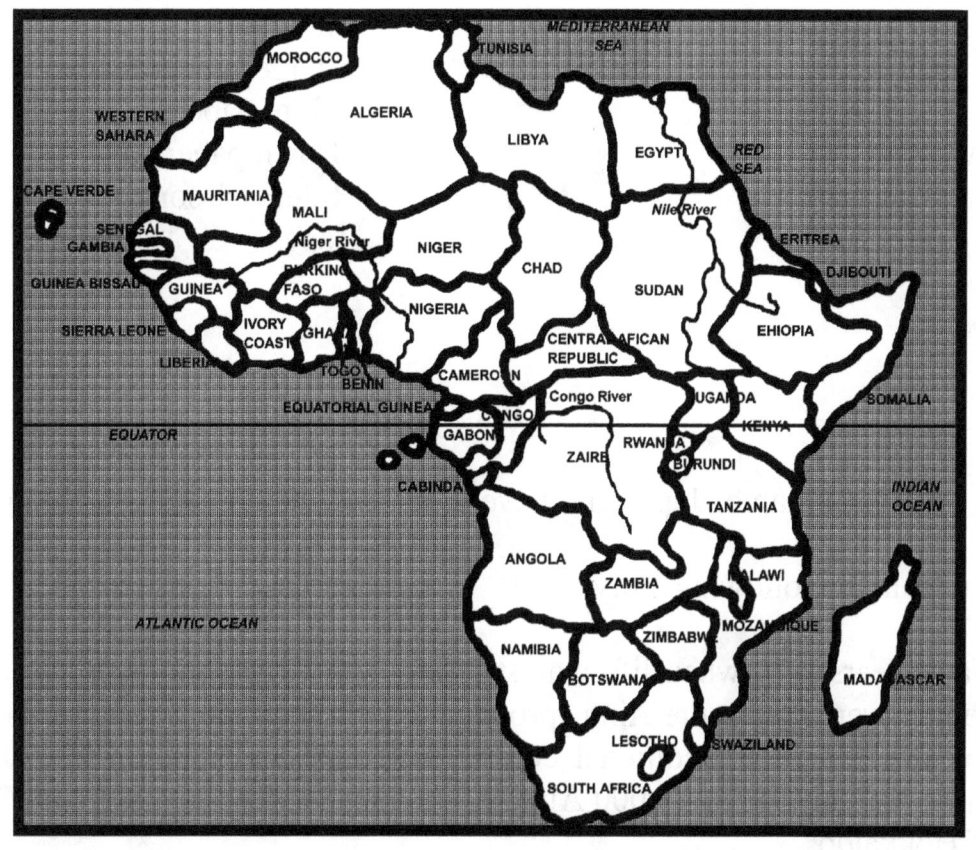

© 2003 Humanics Learning. From *Music Around the World* by Jessica Gates Fredricks

Utuwaskarap
Oki Kano
Japan

Core Connections

Grade 5: Feudal Japan — Geography
        Pacific Ocean, Sea of Japan
        Four main islands: Hokkaido, Honshu (largest), Shikoku, Kyushu
        Tokyo

Materials

Movement activity
Recording of Utuwaskarap
Map of Japan
Globe
Paper towel roll
Crayons

Craft activity
Shoe box
5 large rubber bands
White paper
Brown paper bag
Ruler, scissors
Tape

Procedure

1. Show students a map of Japan and have them find the country on a globe.

2. Tell students the following story:

    Many years ago, when life was still new, the first inhabitants of Japan lived. These people were called the Ainu (pronounced : I-new), and because they lived so long ago, much of their traditional culture, language and religion has disappeared. Today there are only about 24,000 Ainu left in Japan. Most of these Ainu live on the island of Hokkaido.

Traditionally, Ainu men grew very thick beards. Ainu women had tattoos around the mouth that were designed to look like mustaches. The Ainu dressed in bark cloth or skin drapes, and their clothes were often decorated with geometric designs. They were hunters, fishermen, and trappers. The Ainu religion said that spirits and gods inhabited things found in nature, such as stones, water, and trees.

The remaining Ainu strive to maintain their traditions, including the rich musical history of their people. One instrument played by the Ainu is the tankori, a five-stringed instrument made of wood. You may be saying that five-stringed instruments are not unusual, but the Ainu believe that the tankori is a living thing, complete with a heart and a bellybutton!

One modern tankori artist is Oki Kano. Oki did not discover he was part Ainu until he was an adult. He is trying to recreate ancient musical traditions of the Ainu that have been lost for many years, but the only way to truly recreate ancient traditions is to increase the number of people performing the traditions.

3. Tell students you are going to play some modern Ainu music and play the recording. Facilitate a discussion on what sounds different from the music they listen to, and what sounds the same.

4. Using the tankori and vest from the craft activity, invite students to play along with the recording. Before beginning the recording a second time, divide student into two lines and have them stand in those lines facing forward. As they play, the columns should move slowly together, then slowly apart, with tiny steps all the while.

Craft Activity: Make a Tankori and Ainu Vest

Students can make a tankori from a shoebox, some rubber bands and a paper towel roll. The Ainu vest can be made from a brown paper bag, crayons, rulers, and scissors.

Teacher preparation

Have students bring in a shoebox, a brown paper bag and a paper towel roll.

Student directions

Tankori

1. Tape the lid onto the shoebox. Then cut three small rectangle-shaped holes along the width of the box.

2. Cover the box with white paper, making sure to leave the holes open. Stretch five rubber bands around the box longways. Then slide the paper towel roll under the rubber bands at one end of the box.

Vest

3. Open a brown paper grocery bag turn it upside-down. Then cut it so it can be worn as a vest — one large cut down the front, a neck hole in the bottom, and arm holes in each side.

4. The Ainu decorated with geometric designs. Use your ruler to decorate the back of the grocery bag with triangles, rectangles, squares, pentagons, hexagons, and other designs.

5. Use crayons to color the geometric designs, the put the vest on and check for fit.

Japan

Name _____
Date _____

Japan is a country made up of many islands. There are four main islands,
Hokkaido
Honshu
Shikoku
Kyushu

Hokkaido is the northernmost island. Find Hokkaido on the map and label it.
Honshu is the largest island. Find Honshu and label it.
Shikoku is the smallest island. Find Shikoku and label it.
Kyushu is the southenmost island. Find Kyushu and label it.

The **Sea of Japan** is to the west of Honshu. Label the Sea of Japan on your map.
The **Pacific Ocean** is to the east of Honshu. Label the Pacific Ocean on your map.
Tokyo is the capital of Japan. It is located in the middle of Honshu, by the Pacific Ocean. Draw a star to show where Tokyo is on the map.

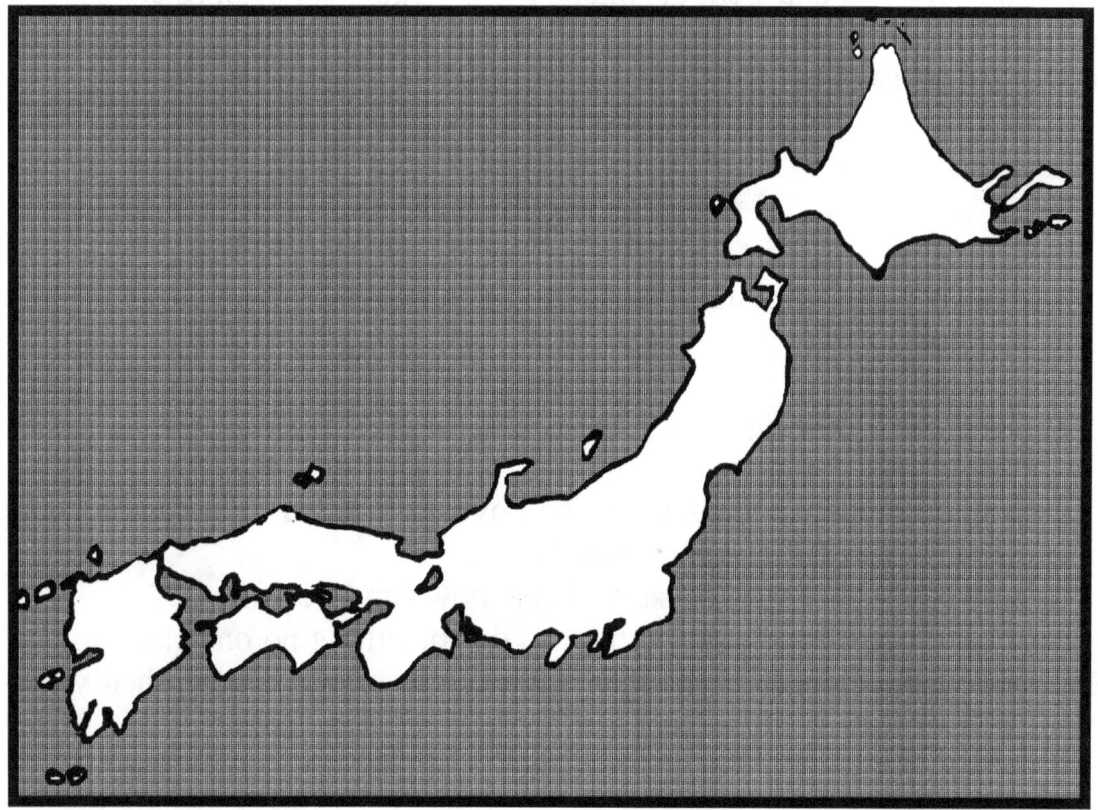

Cumbias
Traditional
Peru

Core Connections

Grade 5: Meso-American Civilizations — Geography
      Identify and locate Central America and South America on maps and globes
      Amazon River, Andes Mountains
      Largest countries in South America: Brazil and Argentina

Materials

Movement activity
Recording of Cumbias
Map of South America and Central America
Globe
Package of Andes candies

Craft activity
Ten large drinking straws
Tape, scissors, ruler
Unlined paper, crayons or markers

Procedure

1. Show students a map of South America and Central America and have them find the areas on a globe.

2. Tell students the following story:

    High in the Andes mountains lived a boy who wanted to be famous more than anything else in the world. His name was Oscar.
    Oscar went to his Papa and said: "Papa, how can I be famous?"
    Papa said: "To be famous you have to do something no one else can do. When you can harvest more caoca beans than anyone else in our village, then you will be famous."

So Oscar practiced harvesting caoca beans. He worked from the time the sun rose until the time the sun set. He went from harvesting three pounds of beans a day to five pounds and finally he was able to harvest 10 pounds of beans a day — and let me tell you, that is a lot of beans!

No one in the village could believe how fast he harvested the beans, because no one else in the village could harvest more than seven pounds a day — and that was if they didn't stop for anything at all, not even lunch.

Oscar went to his Papa and said: "Papa, I can harvest 10 pounds of beans a day. That is something that no one else in the village can do. Why am I not famous yet?"

Papa said: "I do not know."

Then Oscar went to his Mama and said: "Mama, how can I be famous?"

Mama said: "To be famous you have to create something that people want. When you can make something valuable from something very inexpensive, then you will be famous."

So Oscar searched and searched his tiny village for something that was inexpensive. He found sticky sap from a gum tree and banana leaves and all manner of tiny lizards. He tried making clothes for the lizards out of banana leaves, thinking someone would find the lizards valuable if they were wearing leaf jackets, but the clothes didn't fit and the lizards ran away.

Then Oscar searched and searched the nearby mountains for something that was inexpensive. He found sugar cane and caoca beans and delicious pomegranates and all manner of stones. Since there was nothing else to do, he decided to grind the cane and caoca with the stone. He knew it was a waste of time — who would want ground-up cane and caoca?

Oscar's little sister did.

"This tastes great, Oscar," Lolita said, licking the grainy mixture off the grinding stone. "Do you have any more?"

And so Oscar ground up more cane and caoca for his sister and all her friends. The next day there was a large crowd of people waiting outside Oscar's hut.

"We would like to buy some of the magic you ground up for Lolita yesterday," they said.

Oscar frowned. "What magic? I simply ground up what I found in the mountains."

"Whatever it was, it was delicious," said the leader, rubbing his belly. "And we will gladly pay you to make more."

And that was how Oscar became famous — for he found that he could make something valuable and tasty from what no one else wanted after all.

3. Give each student an Andes candy and ask them why they think the company chose the Andes mountains as the logo for their company. What do people think of when

they see a mountain?

4. Play the recording and tell students that the song is dance music from Peru. Invite the students to stand in two rows, facing each other, and learn the following dance steps to the song:

A (repeat 4 times)
   4 steps forward (clap hands with your partner on beat 4)
   4 steps back (clap hands to self on beat 4)

B (repeat 4 times)
   Every other person turns to person on left, claps hands with them 4 times, self 4 times
   Every other person turns to person on right, claps hands with them 4 times, self 4 times

Craft Activity: Make an Andean Pan Pipe

The pan pipe is an ancient wind instrument of the Andes mountains. Students can make one using different lengths of straws.

Teacher preparations

Have each student bring in 10 large drinking straws.

Student directions

1. Lay 8 straws out on your desk. Number them 1 to 8. Leave the first one uncut.

2. Cut a half-inch off the second straw. Cut one inch off the third straw. Cut 1.5 inches off the third straw. Cut 2 inches off the fourth straw. Cut 2.5 inches off the fifth straw. Cut 3 inches off the sixth straw. Cut 3.5 inches off the seventh straw. Cut 4 inches off the eighth straw.

3. Arrange the straws in order from 1 to 8. Then cut the last two straws into eight equal pieces and lay one cut piece between each numbered straw for spacing.

4. Tape the pipes and spacers together so that the tops of the pipes are all at the same height.

5. Cover the pan pipes with white paper and decorate them with crayons. Blow across the top of the pipes as you would an empty bottle to hear the music of the Andes!

Meso-American Geography

Name _____
Date _____

    The Meso-Americans lived in Central America and South America long ago. The Mayans, Incas, and Aztecs are all part of Meso-American civilization.
    The Incas ruled an empire stretching along the Pacific coast of South America. The largest countries in South America are Brazil and Argentina.
    The largest mountain range on the continent of South America are the Andes Mountains. The greatest river in South America is the Amazon River.

Answer the questions by filling in the blank.
1. The Incan empire stretched along the coast of what continent? _____

2. What are the two largest countries in South America?
_____   _____

3. What is the greatest river in South America? _____

On the map:
Trace the **Amazon River** with a blue crayon.
Trace the **Andes Mountains** with a brown crayon.
Draw yellow stripes through **Brazil.**
Draw orange stripes through **Argentina.**

© 2003 Humanics Learning. From *Music Around the World* by Jessica Gates Fredricks

Redentor
Alex Acuna
Peru

Core Connections

Grade 5: Meso-American Civilizations — The Incas
    Ruled an empire stretching along the Pacific coast of South America
    Built great cities (Machu Picchu, Cuzco) high in the Andes mountains

Materials

Movement activity
Recording of Redentor
Map of Peru and South America
Globe
Large open space on floor

Craft activity
Toilet paper tubes
Cereal box
Glue or tape
Construction paper, crayons

Procedure

1. Show students a map of Peru and South America and have them find the country and its continent on a globe.

2. Tell students the following story:

    Once upon a time there live a girl named Juanita. She lived high in the Andes mountains in the city of Cuzco. Juanita was a nice girl and she did well enough in her studies, but she was an explorer at heart.
    Juanita loved to go climbing in the Andes — and not just the small peaks that were close by her city that everyone else enjoyed climbing. No, Juanita loved to climb the highest peaks she could find.
    Her mother said: "You shouldn't climb so high, Juanita — you might fall!"
    And Juanita laughed because everyone knew she was the best climber in the

whole city — she never fell!

Her father said: "You shouldn't climb so high, Juanita — you might be mistaken by the Sky God for a condor and lifted to heaven."

And Juanita laughed because everyone knew the Sky God could never mistake a person for a condor — people had no wings!

Her brother said: "You shouldn't climb so high, Juanita — you will run out of air."

And Juanita laughed because everyone knew you couldn't run out of air!

One day Juanita came to the highest mountain of the Andes — Aconcagua. The mountain was so high that when she looked up, she could not see the top of it. She told her family she was going to climb it, and they told her not to go.

Juanita wouldn't listen. As she climbed, she noticed that it was getting harder to breathe. The air seemed thinner up here.

But did Juanita let that stop her? Of course not! She just kept right on climbing, even though she felt as if she could not get any air into her lungs. It was one thing for Mother and Father to be right, but for her little brother to be right about running out of air? It was unthinkable!

Suddenly Juanita came to the top of the mountain and she looked around — she could see for miles! And since she wasn't concentrating on climbing, she realized that her chest felt as if it was on fire. She tried to take a breath of air and couldn't — it was like there wasn't any air up here at all!

She tried to yell for help, but there was no air to fill her lungs. She grabbed her throat and passed out, sure she would die on top of Aconcagua.

At the base of the mountain, Mother, Father and Brother couldn't see Juanita but knew that she was in trouble. Father called three condors and the family rode the giant birds to the top of Aconcagua, where they found Juanita almost dead. They carried her to the base of the mountain, and as soon as she woke up they scolded her for twenty years.

3. Divide the students into four groups: Mothers, Fathers, Brothers, and Juanitas. Tell the Mothers to clasp their hands, the Fathers to flap their wings like condors, the Brothers to point to the sky, and the Juanitas to frown in disbelief. Each group must remain this way as they act out the piece under your direction. Then run through the piece and cue each group as listed. (When one group is moving, the other remains still.) After the first run-through, have the students switch parts so everyone gets a chance to be each character.

:00	Juanita boasts
:19	Mother wags finger, Father flaps arms
:39	Brother points to sky
:59	Juanita boasts

1:06 Mother wags finger, Father flaps arms
1:27 Brother points to sky
1:50 Juanita boasts
2:06 Juanita climbs, realizes she has no air
2:40 Mom, Dad, Brother wag fingers like "I told you so!"
2:52 Juanita falls to floor, Mom, Dad, Brother fly up and carry her down
3:45 Mom, Dad, Brother return her to ground safely, wag fingers with cymbal crashes

Craft Activity: Make a Meso-American Temple

Students can build an ancient temple to further their studies on Meso-American civilizations. Check out books with pictures of Meso-American temples from the school library for students to get an idea of what they're building. It works best to put students in teams of three or four so that they have more supplies to build with.

Teacher preparation

Have each student team bring in toilet paper tubes, paper towel rolls and cereal or other small boxes. These will be used to build the body of the temple.

Student directions

1. You will build a temple based on the picture your teacher shows you. Use the cereal box for the base and attach cardboard tubes on the sides for variety.

2. Be sure to cover your materials with black, brown or grey paper so they look like dirt, wood or stone.

3. Use construction paper to add trees or bushes around the base of the temple.

The Incas

Name _____
Date _____

The **Incas** were a group of people who lived long ago. Their civilization stretched along the **Pacific coast** of **South America**. They built great cities like **Machu Picchu** and **Cuzco**. These cities were high in the **Andes mountains**, where the air is very thin. Their cities were connected by a system of roads.

Answer the questions below:
1. Which coast did the Incas live along? _____
2. What continent did the Incas live on? _____
3. Name one Incan city: _____
4. What mountains did the Incas live in? _____

On the map:
Find the **Pacific Ocean** and color it blue.
Find **Peru** and color it yellow.
Find the **Amazon River** and trace it with green.
Find the **Andes Mountains** and trace them with brown.

© 2003 Humanics Learning. From *Music Around the World* by Jessica Gates Fredricks

Gnomus from Pictures at an Exhibition
Modeste Mussorgsky
Russia

Core Connections

Grade 5: Russia — Early Growth and Expansion
      Peter the Great
      Moscow and St. Petersburg, Ural Mountains, Siberia
      Baltic Sea, Black Sea, Caspian Sea, Volga River, Don River

Materials

Movement activity
Recording of Pictures at an Exhibition
Map of Russia
Globe
Square-yard pieces of cloth

Craft activity
Shoe box
3 rubber bands
6 toothpicks
White paper

Procedure

1. Show students a map of Russia and have them find the country on a globe.

2. Tell students the following story:

    Once upon a time there was a tiny gnome named Moose. Gnomes are man-shaped creatures who grow to be only 3 feet tall. They live in the forests and wild places of the world, and are rarely seen. They have long white beards, round faces and rosy cheeks, and they like to play tricks on people.

    Moose lived under a tree in the frozen plains of Siberia. Moose was a good gnome, so he played good tricks on people. He put candy bars in the knapsacks of little children so that when they got to school, they found a tasty surprise waiting for them. And sometimes he picked fresh flowers and left them on the desks of very tired teachers who needed to know someone cared.

Unfortunately, not all gnomes were as nice as Moose. Bad gnomes also lived in Siberia, and there were not many creatures who liked to play with bad gnomes. Bad gnomes played very mean tricks on people. They chewed up bubble gum during the day, then sneaked into the houses of little children while they slept and stuck the bubble gum in their hair. When the children woke up, their heads were stuck to the pillows and they had to cry for their mommies to come rescue them! And sometimes the bad gnomes sat by the side of the road, throwing mud at the people passing by. Bad gnomes were bad news, and they didn't have many friends at all.

But there was one gnome no creature wanted to meet, and that was Gnomus. Gnomus was the baddest of the bad. He played the nastiest tricks and said the meanest, unkindest things to the nicest, gentlest creatures.

On this particular day, Gnomus was up to his biggest, baddest trick ever. He had just been to the hut of Baba Yaga for a potion that would make him faster than any other creature alive. But the potion only worked for small amounts of time. Gnomus would peek out from behind a tree, then go sprinting across a frozen Siberian plain faster than a jackrabbit, but he could only do this in short bursts. He traveled across Siberia this way until he came to St. Petersburg, where a great railway had been built.

Gnomus sat beside the tracks, waiting for a train to pass. When the train came, he used his super speed to jump on board. Now he was moving very fast without using his super speed, which was just about used up.

Gnomus sneaked through the passenger cars, through the dining car, and past the coal car into the engine car. He saw that the train conductor had gone to get something to eat. He laughed and told himself this would be his best trick ever. Then he went to the back of the engine car, to the place where the train cars are held together. Thinking mean thoughts, he pulled the pin out of the lock that held the engine car to the rest of the train.

At that moment, the train conductor appeared.

"Hey!" the conductor yelled. "Who are you?"

"My name is Gnomus," said the gnome. Laughing, Gnomus waved the pin in the conductor's face and pointed to the floor where the two train cars were beginning to separate.

"What have you done?" cried the conductor. "You can't leave us here — we'll freeze to death!"

But Gnomus simply waved as he drove away, leaving the conductor and his passengers to die on the frozen plains of Siberia.

3. Play the entire recording of Gnomus (it's very short) and ask students if they were hearing the good gnome or the bad gnome. Review the story and then listen again, identifying how the music is very fast and then stops, just like Gnomus had short

bursts of super speed and then had to stop. Find the place where Gnomus jumps on the train in the music, and talk about the actions that happen.

4. Give each student a square-yard piece of cloth to use as a cape. Then allow them to act out the character of Gnomus to the music, reminding them that they have to stop moving when the music stops, just like Gnomus.

Craft Activity: Make a Balalaika

A balalaika (bal-uh-lie-kuh) is a folk instrument from Russia. It has three strings and is played much like a guitar. Students can make a balalaika using a shoe box, 3 large rubber bands, toothpicks and some paper.

Teacher preparation

Have each student bring in an empty shoe box. Cut a 2-inch by 4-inch rectangular hole in the box. This will be the balalaika's sound hold. When the strings are plucked, the sound will go into the box and resonate.

Student directions

1. Cover the box with white paper. Be sure to leave the hole open.

2. Carefully stretch 3 rubber bands longways around the box.

3. Slide the toothpicks under the rubber bands, about half an inch apart. These will act as the frets for the balalaika.

4. Decorate your balalaika with crayons or markers. Then try playing your favorite song!

Russia

Name _____

    Russia is a country that exists on two continents: Asia and Europe. The capital of Russia is **Moscow**. Draw a circle around Moscow on the map. Another important Russian city is **St. Petersburg**. St. Petersburg was created in 1703 and named after a man called **Peter the Great**. The city is no longer called St. Petersburg — today it is called Leningrad. Find Leningrad on the map and draw a rectangle around it.

    Russia is home to many bodies of water.

    The **Baltic Sea** borders Russia, Finland, and Sweden. Find the Baltic Sea on the map and color it green.

    The **Black Sea** borders Russia and Turkey. Find the Black Sea on the map and color it black.

    The **Caspian Sea** borders Russia and Iran. Find the Caspian Sea on the map and color it blue.

    The Caspian Sea is important because rivers connect to it. There are two important rivers in Russia: the Don River and the Volga River.

    The **Volga River** extends from the top of the Caspian Sea and arches slightly towards the Black Sea. Draw a red line showing the Volga River on the map.

    The **Don River** branches off the Volga River and heads north towards the Arctic Ocean. Draw a green line showing the Don River on the map.

    Some parts of Russia are covered with mountains. The **Ural Mountains** extend north from the Caspian Sea towards the Arctic Ocean. Find the Caspian Sea and then draw triangles to show where the Ural Mountains are on the map.

    Other parts of Russia are covered with snow and ice. The ground is frozen and very few plants or animals live there. This place is called **Siberia**. Siberia is located near the Arctic Circle. On the map, find the Arctic Circle and draw a square around it.

© 2003 Humanics Learning. From *Music Around the World* by Jessica Gates Fredricks

The Hut of Baba Yaga from Pictures at an Exhibition Modeste Mussourgsky Russia

Core Connections

Grade 5: Russia — History and Culture
    Ivan III (the Great)
    Ivan IV (the Terrible); czar (from the Latin "Caesar")
    Peter the Great; modernizing and "Westernizing" Russia

Materials

Movement activity
Recording of Pictures at an Exhibition
Map of Russia
Globe

Craft activity
Brown paper bag, glue
Plastic milk caps, crayons
Metal soda can flip-tops, scissors

Procedure

1. Show students a map of Russia and have them find the country on a globe.

2. Tell students the following story:

    Once upon a time in the highest peaks of the Ural Mountains lived a terrible witch named Baba Yaga. She was a mean, nasty old thing who snuck down into the nearby villages to steal little children out of their beds. Then she would drag them back to her hut in the mountains.
    You may wonder why no one came to help the children — surely they screamed as she dragged them out from their warm covers and into the snowy Russian night? And the truth is that they screamed and screamed and screamed, and no one heard them

because Baba Yaga was the most powerful of all witches, so powerful that she cast a sleeping spell on the entire village. The spell made the entire village sleep so deep that they couldn't hear a thing — not even the screams of a child being dragged from a bed.

One day Baba Yaga became very sick, and because she was a witch, her sickness lasted for five years. And in those five years, she could not use her magic to put a sleeping spell on the village because she had to use all her magic to confuse small birds and animals to wander into her house so she could eat them.

Now, magic is a funny thing — it only works as long as you believe in it. And over time, the people in the village began to forget all about the strange person who lived in the hills. The people forgot why they had been scared to go to sleep at night — once the children stopped disappearing, everybody was happy.

Everybody except Baba Yaga.

On the day she finally recovered from her sickness — five years, two months and thirteen days, to be exact — she couldn't wait for night to fall so she could steal a child.

As the moon rose over the Ural Mountains that night, Baba Yaga snuck down to the village. She cast her spell and waited for the villagers to fall asleep.

But no one did!

"Blast!" muttered Baba Yaga, as she crept back to her hut.

Baba Yaga was still hungry the next day as she watched the children leave the village to play in the thick forests around her hut.

"How nice of the little children to come to me," muttered Baba Yaga. She snuck behind a tree and watched the children playing. They threw frisbees and played catch and picked flowers, and none of them seemed very bothered that a witch was spying on them!

Baba Yaga stepped out from behind the tree and grinned nastily, baring her dirty green teeth. "It's time for dinner, children!" She took a step towards the nearest child.

All the children screamed and ran.

But wait — they weren't running away — they were running towards her! Something strange had happened to these children. They weren't afraid of her. In fact, they were running towards her and looked like they might be a little hungry themselves.

And what do you think happened next?

Listen and decide for yourself!

3. Play the recording and listen for the three distinct sections of the piece (A-B-A). The sinister-sounding beginning is Baba Yaga peering at the children; the pleasant, frolicking-sounding middle is the children playing; the final section is the children fleeing Baba Yaga. Ask students to close their eyes and imagine what's going on. Then have them write down what they think happened in the final section of the story.

4. Divide students into two groups: Baba Yagas and children. Then have students act out the story under your direction while the recording plays a second time.

5. Have students switch parts and act out the piece again so that everyone gets to play both parts.

Craft Activity: Make a Czar Crown

Students can make a crown like the Russian czars wore to assist with their study of Russian rulers.

Teacher preparation

Have each student bring in a large assortment of plastic milk caps, as many different colors as possible. It is also helpful to have some of the metal soda can flip-tops. These will serve as jewels in the crown, and the paper bag will form the body of the crown.

Student directions

1. Cut the bottom off the paper bag, then make a cut up one side so that it is completely flat. Then fold it in half long-ways. The side that is open is the bottom of your crown.

2. Get a friend to help you wrap the bag around your head like a crown so it fits snugly, then tape it closed. Cut triangles out of the top so that the crown has points on top.

3. Glue different colored milk caps to your crown to represent jewels. Add some metal soda can flip-tops for a glittering effect.

Russian Rulers

Name _____
Date _____

Russia has had many rulers over the years.

Ivan III was known as Ivan the Great. He ruled from 1440 to 1504. When he took over, Russia belonged to the Tatar rulers. Ivan the Great declared independence from the Tatars in 1480. He was also responsible for improving buildings, construction of new churches, and making artillery-proof walls for cities. He had a son named Ivan IV.

Ivan IV was known as Ivan the Terrible. He ruled from 1530 to 1584. He was the first formal tzar (or czar, pronounced "zar") of Russia. The title czar is from the Roman imperial title "Caesar". Ivan the Terrible was known for being brutal. Although he expanded Russia, he also brought it to near ruin.

Peter the Great ruled from 1672 to 1725. He was responsible for modernizing and "Westernizing" Russia. Peter the Great did many fine things — built roads and canals, modernized the army and navy, and secured seaports for trade. He created a Grand Embassy that traveled to other European countries to find the best people. His embassy then recruited these people to work for Russia.

Answer the questions.

1. Which Russian ruler declared independence from the Tatar invaders?
a) Ivan III   **b) Ivan IV**   **c) Peter the Great**

2. Which Russian ruler was responsible for "Westernizing" Russia?
a) Ivan III   **b) Ivan IV**   **c) Peter the Great**

3. Which Russian ruler was the first formal tzar or czar?
a) Ivan III   **b) Ivan IV**   **c) Peter the Great**

4. Which Russian ruler secured seaports for trade?
a) Ivan III   **b) Ivan IV**   **c) Peter the Great**

5. Which Russian ruler was known as "the Terrible"?
a) Ivan III   **b) Ivan IV**   **c) Peter the Great**

6. Which Russian ruler made artillery-proof walls for cities?
a) Ivan III   **b) Ivan IV**   **c) Peter the Great**

7. Russia invaded Novgorod in 1472. Who was the ruler at that time?
a) Ivan III   **b) Ivan IV**   **c) Peter the Great**

8. The Grand Embassy was formed in 1697. Who was ruling Russia at that time?
a) Ivan III   **b) Ivan IV**   **c) Peter the Great**

© 2003 Humanics Learning. From *Music Around the World* by Jessica Gates Fredricks

La Virgen de la Macarena
Traditional
Spain

Core Connections

Grade 4: Geography of Western Europe
    Iberian Peninsula, Spain and Portugal, Mediterranean Sea, Atlantic Ocean

Grade 5: European Exploration
    Magellan crosses the Pacific; one ship returns to Spain, making the first round-the-world voyage

Materials

Movement activity
Recording of La Virgen de la Macarena
Pieces of red cloth or red paper to use as a cape
Map of Spain
Globe

Craft activity
Paper towel tubes
dry rice or beans
plastic milk caps
tape

Procedure

1. Show students a map of Spain and have them find the country on a globe.

2. Tell students the following story:

    Once upon a time there was a very cocky bullfighter named Pedro. Pedro wasn't afraid of anyone or anything, and he certainly wasn't afraid of bulls. He was one of the best bullfighters in Spain.
    "Pedro will fight any bull," said the townspeople of Madrid. "He's crazy."
    "I'm not crazy," Pedro always muttered. "Is it crazy to do what I love?"
    Pedro loved fighting bulls. He loved to taunt the bull with his big red cape. The

bull would stomp his hooves and shake his mighty head before charging at him, and Pedro's favorite part of the fight was when he jumped easily out of the way, allowing the bull to go charging madly past him.

People brought their bulls from all across Spain to Madrid. They wanted to watch Pedro fight the bulls, for it was said that whoever owned a bull that beat Pedro would receive a large sum of money. One day a woman no one knew appeared in the town plaza, ringing a bell. "Good people of Madrid, I have found a bull with terrible speed and sharp horns. This bull is ready to fight. Where is the one you call Pedro?"

The townspeople led the woman towards the place where Pedro fought bulls. As they walked through the town, people heard the news and followed, until a great band of people arrived at the ring and clamored for the great bull fighter.

The woman led her bull into the ring and closed the gate.

Pedro was so excited about the new bull that he grabbed a blue tablecloth instead of his fine red cape and ran towards the gate. He stepped into the ring and pulled his black cap tightly down on his head. He stared the bull in the eyes and stepped towards the center of the ring, swirling the blue tablecloth and calling torro, torro!

But the bull did not move.

Pedro danced towards the bull, calling torro and swirling the tablecloth. He danced in front of the bull, behind the bull, towards the bull, and away from the bull, but the bull did not move.

Then Pedro took off his black cap and threw it in the dust, saying, "How can I fight a bull who does not move? I think this bull is asleep!"

Suddenly, the bull stamped his hooves and swung his great head back and forth, sharp horns glinting in the sun. He snorted and thundered towards Pedro in a cloud of dust.

Ahhh, thought Pedro as he twirled the tablecloth left and right, now we will see what you can do. Pedro twirled his tablecloth left and right, but the bull was not looking at his tablecloth. The bull was looking right at Pedro's hair, which was reddish-orange and very bright. Pedro threw the tablecloth far away from him, but the bull kept coming. Pedro began to run, and the bull chased him. The bull was big, but Pedro was a very fast runner, and the two ran around the ring for two days before they became too tired to run anymore.

3. Before playing the recording, tell students that cocky Pedro is represented by the trumpet sound (high), and the big bull is represented by the tuba sound (low). Ask them to imagine how the bullfight looks while the music is playing. Then play the recording.

4. Divide students into teams of two, with one student playing the part of the bull and the other playing the part of Pedro. Have them act out the stories to the music.

Craft Activity: Make a Rain Stick

A rain stick is a musical instrument that makes the sound of the rain. They are made from skeletons of dead cacti or bamboo that had been dried in the sun. You can make one using a paper towel roll, 2 plastic milk caps, about 20 toothpicks, and some dry rice.

Rain sticks are associated with the continent of South America, which is what Magellan sailed around on his voyage around the world. Have students find the Strait of Magellan on a map and trace his voyage from Spain and back again.

Teacher preparation

Have students bring in empty paper towel rolls. Make cuts in the sides so that students can pass a toothpick through a slit in one side and out the other. The ends of the toothpick will should stick out either side. When students put rice into the tube and turn it upside down, it will hit the toothpicks and make the sound of falling rain.

Student directions

1. Close one end of the cardboard tube with a plastic milk cap and secure the cap with tape.

2. Push toothpicks through the slits in the empty paper towel tube. Make sure the ends of the toothpick can be seen on both sides of the cardboard tube.

3. Put a quarter cup of dry rice or beans into the cardboard tube. It should make a neat sound as it falls through the tube hitting the toothpicks on the way down.

4. Close the other end of the tube with a plastic milk cap and secure the cap with tape.

5. Tip the rain stick upside down and listen to the sound of the rain as the rice falls!

Spain

Name _____
Date _____

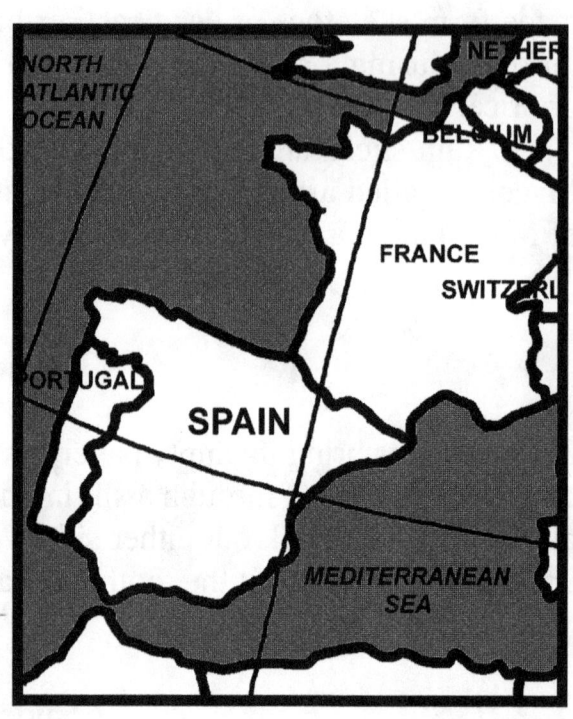

Spain is a country in Europe. It is located on the **Iberian Peninsula** in the far southwest corner of Europe.

But Spain is not the only country on the Iberian Peninsula. If you look at the west end of the Iberian Peninsula, you will see a small country called **Portugal**.

On the map to your right, color Spain red. Then use a yellow crayon to color Portugal.

Two major bodies of water surround the Iberian Peninsula — the **Atlantic Ocean** and the **Mediterranean Sea**. Color both of these waters blue.

Ferdinand Magellan was a Portugese ship captain. He wanted to sail around the world, but the king of Portugal didn't believe it was possible. So Magellan went to the king of Spain. The king of Spain liked Magellan and gave him ships to make the voyage.

He sailed around the bottom of the South American continent, through a place now known as the Straight of Magellan. He crossed the **Pacific Ocean**. He was killed in the Phillipines, and only one of his ships returned to Spain. But the ship's return — with just 18 crew members alive — marked the first round-the-world voyage.

Fill in the blank to answer questions from the information above.

1. Spain and Portugal are part of the _____ Peninsula.

2. A body of water to the east of Spain is the _____ Sea.

3. The country of _____ is on the west end of the Iberian Peninsula.

4. The ocean west of the Iberian Peninsula is the _____ Ocean.

5. Ferdinand _____ was a Portugese ship captain.

6. One of Magellan's ships made the first round-the-_____ voyage.

© 2003 Humanics Learning. From *Music Around the World* by Jessica Gates Fredricks

Common Core Standards Correlations

National Child Assessment Form
Music Around the World

This document is a correlation of the skills presented in *Music Around the World* to the skills that are assessed on the National Child Assessment Form. This assessment form is used to determine whether students are ready both developmentally and intellectually to move into kindergarten. This correlation indicates where the skills that will be assessed are presented in this book. The number of skills presented in the books in this series will increase with an increase in children's ages, development levels, and intellect.

Social Emotional Development

1. Identifies body parts ....
2. Shows feeling 50
3. Separates from parents ....
4. Relates to adults ....
5. Interacts with children 1-4, 9-20, 25-49, 54-61
6. Seeks new experiences 1-4, 13-16, 25-29
7. Maintains interest 1-61
8. Plays cooperatively 1-4, 9-61
9. Modulates voice 17-20
10. Persists in task 5-8, 13-53, 58-61
11. Shows pride ....
12. Shows social awareness 44-45
13. Protects self ....
14. Concerned about fairness ....
15. Demonstrates responsibility ....
16. Aware of consequences ....
17. Shows creativity 1-61
18. Exhibits appropriate values ....

Language Development

19. Follows directions (simple) 1-61
20. Extended listening 1-61
21. Follows directions (multiple) 1-61
22. Discriminates between words ....
23. Labels objects 9-12

24. Speaks informally ....
25. Initiates conversation 45
26. Speaks more extensively ....
27. Asks questions ....
28. Uses prepositions ....
29. Uses adjectives ....
30. Exhibits auditory memory ....
31. Sequencing and retelling ....
32. Exhibits reading interest ....
33. Knows reading progression ....
34. Knows alphabet ....
35. Uses imagination 1-4, 9-12, 17-61
36. Plays roles 1-4, 9-12, 17-29, 34-61

Cognitive Development

37. Visual discrimination with colors 5-8, 17-29, 34-45, 50-53, 58-61
38. Identifies shapes ....
39. Classifies objects 30-33, 58-61
40. Understands number concepts ....
41. Knows the five senses 13-16
42. Draws a person (outline) 1-4
43. Compares length ....
44. Compares size ....
45. Understands numbers ....
46. Detects a pattern ....
47. Understands relative qualities ....
48. Understands numbers ....
49. Knows seasons 9-12
50. Draws a person (details) 1-4
51. Classifies objects (matching set to use) ....
52. Recognizes fantasy 1-4, 54-57
53. Recognizes cause and effect 58-61
54. Predicts outcomes 58-61

Motor Skills Development

55. Walks on tiptoes 9-12, 17-20, 58-61
56. Walks balance board ....
57. Jumps from stool ....
58. Hops on one foot 9-12, 17-20, 58-61
59. Catches ball (12" diameter) ....
60. Throws ball ....
61. Balances on one foot 9-12, 17-20
62. Works puzzle (3 pieces) ....
63. Copies a circle and a cross ....
64. Gallops 1-4, 46-53
65. Dances 9-12, 17-20, 30-45, 58-61
66. Explores space 9-12, 17-20
67. Works puzzle (5 pieces) ....

68. Uses scissors ....
69. Copies letters ....
70. Skips ....
71. Catches ball (3-4" diameter)..
72. Walks backward ....

Hygiene and Self-Development

73. Allows sufficient time for toilet needs ....
74. Dresses self (basic)...
75. Knows identifying information ....
76. Uses spoon and fork ....
77. Puts things away ....
78. Cleans spills ....
79. Plays actively 1-4, 9-12, 17-20, 25-29, 34-61
80. Manages bathroom facilities...
81. Dresses self (buttons and zippers) ....
82. Helps prepare for activity 54-56
83. Cares for toys..
84. Cares for possessions ....
85. Tries new food ....
86. Identifies food..
87. Demonstrates judgment 3-12
88. Recognizes weather 9-12
89. Understands travel ....
90. Knows address and telephone number ....

142

Head Start Kindergarten Readiness Assessment
Music Around the World

This document is a correlation of the skills presented in *Music Around the World* to the skills that are assessed on the Head Start Readiness Assessment. This assessment form is used to determine whether students are ready both developmentally and intellectually to move into kindergarten. This correlation indicates where the skills that will be assessed are presented in this book. The number of skills presented in the books in this series will increase with an increase in children's ages, development levels, and intellect.

A. Academics

1. Recognizes letters ....
2. Recognizes shapes ....
3. Recognizes colors 5-8, 17-29, 34-45, 50-53, 58-61
4. Counts 10 objects ....
5. Writes own first name ....
6. Can recognize rhyming words ....

B. Self-Regulation

1. Comforts self ....
2. Pays attention 1-56, 58-61
3. Controls impulses ....
4. Follow directions 1-8, 13-61
5. Negotiates solutions ....
6. Plays cooperatively 1-4, 9-57
7. Participates in circle time 1-4
8. Handles frustration well ....

C. Social Expression

1. Expresses empathy ....
2. Relates well to adults ....
3. Has expressive abilities 1-4, 13-57
4. Is curious and eager to learn ....
5. Expresses needs and wants ....
6. Engages in symbolic play 1-4, 9-57

D. Self-Care and Motor Skills

1. Use of small manipulatives 5-29, 46-53
2. Has general coordination 1-4, 9-12, 17-24, 30-61
3. Performs basic self-help/self-care tasks ....

About the Author

Jessica Gates Fredricks has a Bachelor of Music Education Degree from Florida Southern College. She has been a Director of Bands, a Music Specialist, and an Assistant Band Director. She has received awards such as the Teacher to Teacher Connection Developer Grant, the Florida Elementary Music Educators Creativity Grant, the AT&T TeachNet Project Award Winner, the Time Warner Crystal Apple Award, the Bethune Academy Teacher of the Year, the Polk County East Area Educator of the Year, the Top Elementary Program Away of the Disney Teacheriffic Award, and an Outstanding Arts and Culture Program Award from Disney Community Service Awards. In 1999, she founded the Bethune Academy Music Outreach, which provides enior centers with performing student musical groups on a monthly basis. She and her husband, Cole, live in Winter Haven, FL, with their two cats, Sammy and Cleo.

9 780893 343798

www.ingramcontent.com/pod-product-compliance
Lightning Source LLC
Chambersburg PA
CBHW080250170426
43192CB00014BA/2622